Unlo

Credits

Front cover: © Steve Collender – Fotolia

Back cover: © Jakub Semeniuk/iStockphoto.com, © Royalty-Free/
Corbis, © agencyby/iStockphoto.com, © Andy Cook/iStockphoto.
com, © Christopher Ewing/iStockphoto.com, © zebicho – Fotolia.
com, © Geoffrey Holman/iStockphoto.com, ©Photodisc/Getty
Images, © James C. Pruitt/iStockphoto.com, © Mohamed Saber –
Fotolia.com

Unlock Your Creativity

Jenny Hare

Hodder Education

338 Euston Road, London NW1 3BH

Hodder Education is an Hachette UK company

First published in UK 2011 by Hodder Education

This edition published 2011

Copyright © 2011 Jenny Hare

The moral rights of the author have been asserted

Database right Hodder Education (makers)

All rights reserved. No part of this publication may be reproduced, stored in a retrieval system or transmitted in any form or by any means, electronic, mechanical, photocopying, recording or otherwise, without the prior permission in writing of Hodder Education, or as expressly permitted by law, or under terms agreed with the appropriate reprographic rights organization. Enquiries concerning reproduction outside the scope of the above should be sent to the Rights Department, Hodder Education, at the address above.

You must not circulate this book in any other binding or cover and you must impose this same condition on any acquirer.

British Library Cataloguing in Publication Data: a catalogue record for this title is available from the British Library.

10 9 8 7 6 5 4 3 2 1

The publisher has used its best endeavours to ensure that any website addresses referred to in this book are correct and active at the time of going to press. However, the publisher and the author have no responsibility for the websites and can make no guarantee that a site will remain live or that the content will remain relevant, decent or appropriate.

The publisher has made every effort to mark as such all words which it believes to be trademarks. The publisher should also like to make it clear that the presence of a word in the book, whether marked or unmarked, in no way affects its legal status as a trademark.

Every reasonable effort has been made by the publisher to trace the copyright holders of material in this book. Any errors or omissions should be notified in writing to the publisher, who will endeavour to rectify the situation for any reprints and future editions.

Hachette UK's policy is to use papers that are natural, renewable and recyclable products and made from wood grown in sustainable forests. The logging and manufacturing processes are expected to conform to the environmental regulations of the country of origin.

www.hoddereducation.co.uk

Typeset by Cenveo Publisher Services.

Printed in Great Britain by CPI Cox & Wyman, Reading

Also available
in ebook

Contents

Meet the author   ix
In one minute   x
Introduction   xii

1   **What is creativity?**   1
    So many kinds of creativity   1
    Recognizing your own creativity   4
    Recognizing the many sources of creativity   5
    Contacts to fire your creativity   11
    Who is creative?   12
    Do you need talent to be creative?   13
    Opening up your creativity   13
2   **Practical ways to get in touch with your creativity**   16
    Letting in the light of creativity   16
    How to introduce a creative approach into
        your everyday life   18
    Free-flow writing as a daily conduit
        for your creativity   20
    More ways to spark your creativity and keep
        it vibrant   23
    How to live creatively   26
3   **Encouragement**   31
    Appreciation and encouragement   31
    Self-belief – how to adopt, develop and nurture it   33
    The power of focus, thought... and
        then relaxation   36
    Develop the seven principles of creativity   38
    Be your biggest ally and advocate   39
    Take one step...   40
    Creativity loves a challenge   41
    Understanding and defusing
        subjective criticism   42
4   **A creative attitude**   46
    What do *you* think about things?   46
    Developing a creative attitude   49
    Playing creatively   51

Enjoying the creative power of curiosity   52
Appreciating the wonder and mystery
   of the world   54
Choosing a 'what's-right' mindset   55
Thoroughly enjoying being creative!   56
5   **Freeing yourself from the blocks and defences**
that sabotage your creativity   59
Freeing the high self-esteem your creativity
   needs to flourish   59
Managing negative emotions to benefit your
   creativity, not impede it   62
How being creative can heal or even
   pre-empt depression   65
Bringing in positive emotions to light up
   your creativity   67
Embracing practicalities to free you to be creative   68
Sideways thinking about your talents and ambitions   71
Doing different things to free and fire your creativity   72
Letting go of envy and jealousy   73
6   **Finding your muse**   75
Discovering the magic of time   75
Discovering the right place   77
Giving yourself the right tools   80
Discovering the magic of inspirational outings   80
Using all kinds of media to uplift you and give
   you ideas   82
Relishing the creative richness of silence and solitude   84
Letting a beloved human being or pet be your muse   85
7   **Personal contacts**   88
Listening to or talking with like-minded, creative
   people   88
Being part of a team   90
Forging and maintaining a one-to-one creative
   partnership   91
Exercising and playing games and sports with others   93
Making music and dancing   94
Laughing and having fun with others   95
Being creative the way you want to be   96
Buffering and transforming others' negativity   100

8   The right-brain and left-brain effect on creativity   104
     The way the brain works with our creativity   104
     Our emotional/spiritual/imaginative/intuitive side   107
     Our thoughtful/controlling/practical side   114
     The way the right and left sides of our brain
       do a great job in tandem   115
9   Mystical ways to let your creativity come through   117
     The way imagination influences our creativity   117
     How to let your imagination live and soar   118
     The usefulness of boredom   120
     Meditation   123
     Developing a spiritual feeling of connection with the
       creative essence of the world
       and the universe   126
     Listening for inspiration   129
10 Process or product? The joy of creative process
    for its own sake – and how it unlocks your creativity   132
     Being and becoming, moment and meaning   132
     The joy of creative process for its own sake – and
       how it unlocks your creativity   133
     Engaging in the process   135
     Ways to start the process   136
     When you and your creativity are flying together   138
     The joy of an end product   140
     The emotional release of being creatively productive   142
     The healing power of being creative   143
     Being and becoming, moment and meaning (again)   144
11 A lifestyle that nurtures your creativity   147
     Your home is also home to your creativity   147
     How you can use your leisure time creatively   149
     The potentially inspiring interplay between you,
       others and your creativity   152
     The effect your love of life has on your creativity   154
     Creative oases   154
     Using your senses to enhance your creativity   155
     The importance of noticing beauty
       and uniqueness   157
     Everyday creative choices   158

12 The whole spectrum of being creative   **161**

The fulfilment of living creatively   161

The habit of being intuitively creative   162

The surprise, blessing and fun of creative awareness
and the inspiration of ongoing learning   164

How being imaginative and optimistic about your
creativity really does light up your life   166

Listen for your soul's music   168

Reach out to others in your own creative way
and touch them with your verve and happiness   169

The joy of recognizing and standing up for your
true creative self   171

The synchronicity of creativity   172

Taking it further   **175**

Index   **177**

Meet the author

Welcome to *Unlock Your Creativity*!

Writing *Unlock Your Creativity* has been an inspiring, joyful and, of course, deeply thought-provoking time. Each day, as I've sat down to work, whatever my current mood or circumstances, positivity has started to flow as soon as I've started to write. I hope this comes through clearly to you and lights up your path, too.

All through my life I've seen what a difference it makes when we're positive and when we use our creativity. Very noticeably, we feel better. A positive attitude and thoughtful approach lift us out of the shadows if we're feeling down and give us added gladness and often joy when all is well.

Increasingly, as the years have gone by, I've realized that being creative is a choice we can make at any time. As soon as we make that positive choice, a special kind of energy starts to flow along with other feel-good traits such as love, courage, common sense and optimism.

Although cherishing my creativity is habitual for me, I'll still catch myself feeling uncreative sometimes and then I know I need to think positively quickly and firmly. Then, indeed, it feels like putting the lights back on and in an instant my positivity and creativity return. Of course, when I suffer hurt or bereavement, as we are all bound to sometimes, it hits me hard. But even during such down times I never lose sight of the light of positivity and creativity, and I know that what I have to do is let that light back in and it will help me see the path and keep going as positively and constructively as possible.

Your mind is yours and you have a tremendous ability to use it well and to use your creativity to the full. Above all, our creativity can help us see and participate in the goodness and wonder of life, which is so complex, so extraordinary, so full of goodness, beauty and love.

In sharing my experience, thoughts, techniques and tips on creativity, I hope I inspire and help enable you to develop and increase yours. It's an ongoing process and learning curve and it feels wonderful!

In one minute

Deep in your heart, mind and soul you know that you are creative but, for all kinds of reasons, like most of us you probably don't use this amazing ability as much as you would like and perhaps it feels as though it's locked up inside you. The mission of *Unlock Your Creativity* is to free that hidden energy, to give you the keys to being your true creative self.

Through the following chapters we'll look at the various inhibitions and misconceptions that often stop us enjoying our creativity. Recognizing them frees us to see that we are creative in all kinds of ways and can choose to use our ability, enjoy it to the full and, if we wish, develop and polish it.

I'm not living in cloud-cuckoo-land – of course, not all of us can make millions from a creative career, or become the next celebrated genius or icon. But we *are* all imaginative. We *are* all resourceful. We *all* have an extraordinary capacity to be creative in so many diverse ways. Like snowflakes, each of us has our own creative way and being. So let's enjoy it!

In this book we will explore the whole notion of creativity – and how you can unlock yours and live it, love it, use it… to the full.

Each chapter has its own take on creativity, but running through them all will be these essential, inspiring themes: encouragement, self-belief, the sheer pleasure and often joy of letting your creativity live and thrive. Also, I will keep addressing the things that set out to thwart or even put the stopper back on our attempts to free our creativity, and keep giving advice and tips on how to counter these and even use them to help our creativity.

We'll look at easy-to-follow, enjoyable steps that will not only enable you to release your creativity but also help it flow smoothly and joyfully. For, above all, being creative is a hugely *joyful* process. From the moment an original thought or idea arrives in your mind, feel-good hormones start to flow and work alongside your imagination and/or practical plans.

In this book, you'll also be encouraged – goaded even! – to be creative every day, and here again you'll be given lots of suggestions to help you. For the more you pay attention to your creativity and use it, the more easily it will spark and flow.

Every day feel the inspiration, take its hand and dance with it!

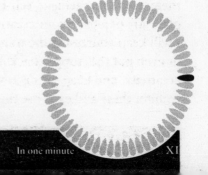

Introduction

Creativity is the essence of life. The way we think and the words we speak are part of our creativity. So is the way we love. The way we dance and sing and walk or run. The way we rage against injustice and grieve for the sorrows of the world and our own losses. The way we make a difference, sometimes against all the odds. The way we work and play. The things we make. Our appreciation of joy and beauty and our perception of sadness and ugliness.

Everything we do is part of our creativity – unless, that is, we go through life on automatic pilot. So let's not do that. Let's be present in every moment. Aware of what's going on, where we are, where we're going, what we're doing. And let us be and progress and do as well as we can, using all our creative ability to make this life, and others' lives, and the world, a better place.

Let's be aware of our connection to all the creativity in this world as we know it and perhaps to other dimensions and worlds beyond or parallel to ours that, as yet, we only sense.

Because of my work, much of my personal experience of creativity is in writing, painting and counselling, but this book is for *everyone* who is creative or longs to be, not just those involved in the arts but people of all kinds and in all walks of life. We are all creative and we can express it in countless ways.

The miracle of our creation is in the energy that fuels us, the love that transports us, the gift of the magic of being creative.

We don't understand this alchemy but we experience it and feel its pulse. It is the living, beating heart of each and every one of us and, indeed, of our world.

Sometimes it is locked up inside us.

Unlock it and set it free to light up your life.

1

What is creativity?

In this chapter you will learn:
- *about the many different ways we can be creative*
- *how to recognize your own creativity*
- *to appreciate the many sources of creativity*
- *about the myth of who is and who isn't creative*
- *how to open up your creativity.*

So many kinds of creativity

Creativity is beguiling and exciting for us all because it comes in so many forms, with all kinds of aspects and facets – when we give our creativity a chance to flow, energy and feel-good hormones begin to surge through us.

There really are myriad ways you can be creative and it's inspiring to run through them every now and then to remind yourself of your wide-ranging creative scope. As you do, notice any of special interest to you, any that seem to shine and any that make you feel pleased as you find yourself thinking: 'Yes – that's me!'

Probably the first thing that comes to mind about creativity is **imagination**. We have it in bucketfuls when we're children. As a kid living in the suburbs, I liked to dream of other places. I had an imaginary farm in the country with several horses and ponies and all sorts of other animals. And there was an ancient city, too – I'd imagine going back in time and walking in the streets, looking in the windows and going into the shops, and I'd feel how it would be to live in the busy heart of a town.

Can you remember how vivid your imagination was when you were little? Go back to that time and see if you can remember how you played – especially when you were on your own – and if you invented imaginary settings or worlds. Now you're an adult, do you still give your imagination a chance to play and stretch itself? If you do, your creativity will love it and thrive.

Daydreaming is fabulously creative. We create another dimension and live in it for a while. Again, remember how easy it was to daydream when you were small. Did you talk to your toys? Did you have imaginary friends? And did you ever have imaginary conversations or adventures with the people in your real world, too? Shut your eyes and remember how absorbing your imaginative play was and the twofold pleasure of it – not only the delight in the things you imagined, but also how good it felt to let your creativity flow.

If you've never stopped daydreaming, that's great. But if you were schooled out of it by teachers who were anxious to follow the curriculum and couldn't see its value and potential, then give yourself permission to start again. Daydreaming is a rich seam of imaginative gold that lets your creativity flow – we'll look at this again in Chapter 9.

Being creative is also often taken to mean someone is naturally **original** and **very individual**. And so we all are. Each of us is a one-off blueprint. You're not the same as anyone else – you have a unique personality and your own kind of innate creativity. Isn't it extraordinary to think that you are totally distinct from anyone else and that so is your creative flair? Enjoy the thought – it's true. Moreover, you can foster your unique identity and your ability to think originally, too, and make more of these gifts.

You'll also have your own kind of **ingenuity** – the way you approach everyday situations, look at problems and think about how to solve them. And you are inherently extremely resourceful – you have so many diverse abilities that you use to cope with life. All this is part of your creative ability to manage your life and navigate its many paths.

Creativity also encompasses the ability for **invention**. We tend to think of inventors as being unusual in their talent to come up with completely new concepts. And so they are. But, again, so are you. You probably have all sorts of ideas that you could, if you decided to, develop and follow through. But even just thinking about them nurtures the inventiveness you were born with and still have – it's fun and it's an exciting part of your creativity.

Inspiration! This is another wonderful part of being creative. Whenever you have that lovely feeling of being spontaneously inspired to do something, or someone makes you feel really excited about a possibility or your potential, or you find yourself inspiring others, the inspiration ignites your creativity.

Your creativity may manifest itself in the way you **gather and sort information**, process ideas and tasks, and organize other people, too. It may express itself in the way you approach your work, finding the most positive ways to enjoy it and do it well. It's about looking for the extra edge – the energy and flow with which we can approach anything – *if* we decide to do so.

Some people are great at coming up with **ideas**. Actually we all are, *if* we encourage ourselves. I love to ask people to 'brainstorm' ideas and then listen fascinated as even those who claim not to be creative come up with some really good ones.

And then there's **insight**. Being able to understand something previously unnoticed or even hidden means you're looking at things in a different way.

For some, it's the **planning** of a project that's creatively fulfilling. You may get a great creative buzz from conjuring up an overview vision of how it's going to be, take pleasure in looking at the steps that will take you there, or just love getting stuck into the detail of every part of your plan. Review any project you've handled yourself or been involved in – what did it mean to you and how did it inspire your creative input?

We can always put our **individual slant** on something, thinking sideways – in popular terms, 'thinking out of the box'. When you look at something afresh and bring your creativity to it, you'll often come up with a different or even completely new approach to it or method of organizing or doing it.

Perhaps most often associated with creativity is **artistic, sensual** ability – the creativity of visual artists, for example, and of musicians, composers, dancers and writers. The creativity of athletes and sportsmen and women comes in here, too.

The creative spark is always there in us – it never dies. We may use it barely at all – and yet any of these elements of creativity can fan it so it glows with life, staying bright all through our lives.

Recognizing your own creativity

When you're being creative, in any of the many diverse ways we'll look at throughout this book, you'll feel a certain wonderful kind of energy flowing into, through and out of you – and all around you, too. It's a stunning feeling – not like anything else. So often we're just not aware of it, or don't pay attention to it. So one of the first ways to encourage your creativity is to start recognizing and registering it. 'Yes – there it is – I can feel it flowing!'

Try this

Tick any of the following **creativity statements** that are true of you:

▶ I'm imaginative
▶ I love daydreaming
▶ I like being original
▶ I'm rather ingenious
▶ I like seeing the beauty in all sorts of things
▶ I like having a nice home
▶ I sometimes – or often – feel full of inspiration
▶ I like to gather and sort information
▶ I enjoy making things
▶ I like to approach work and other things my own way
▶ I'm a great parent
▶ I like inventing things
▶ I'm a good leader
▶ I'm a good team member
▶ I like working on my own
▶ I often have ideas
▶ I love planning a project and putting it together
▶ I'm artistic
▶ I like thinking about things
▶ I enjoy problem-solving
▶ I'll often have special insights

- ▶ I like to put my individual slant on things – thinking 'sideways' or 'out of the box'
- ▶ I'm funny and love making people laugh
- ▶ I like to make the best of my appearance and look as nice as possible.

Make a **list of the statements** you've ticked and keep it safe to remind you of your wealth of creativity and to inspire you to use it.

Insight

By becoming alert to the amazing scope of your creativity, you'll allow it to manifest itself more and more in your daily life. If you say, like so many do, 'I'm not creative,' you unintentionally hold your creativity back because you are not giving it the encouragement it needs to breathe. But as soon as you think about the various ways you are naturally creative, and realize that you can encourage them of your own volition, you set your creativity free and allow yourself to welcome its presence in your life and encourage it with your appreciation and joy.

Recognizing the many sources of creativity

In our genetic make-up, we are each given the capacity to think for ourselves and use our willpower. You have the ability to look at the potential scope of your creativity and approach it individually in the mix that's particularly right for you. Perhaps some people have more ready-to-run creativity than others, but we can all hug the innate creativity we all have with joy and thankfulness. We can all see how nurture works hand in hand with nature, bringing creativity on and encouraging it to thrive and develop, inspiring it to dance and even soar.

Think of a genius and you'll see someone who took their genetic ability and developed it with determination, practice, learning, perseverance and, above all, passion. Creativity, just like, but perhaps more than, any of our other genetic abilities, responds to love and enthusiasm, care and attention, and rewards us by lighting up our lives. So take yours happily in your own hands and look after it well. However you use it – simply and quietly or taking it to its full potential in the pursuit of greater challenges – it will bring you much pleasure and joy.

For many years creativity has been associated with **right brain function**, while the left side of the brain has been linked to logic. Although this idea is interesting, it's important that we don't make broad generalizations. There's no such thing as a 'right-brain person' or a 'left-brain person' – we all use both sides and it's crucial, I believe, not to be formulaic about where the different brain functions originate. The fact is, 'creative people' can be logical and 'logical people' can be creative.

However, there is definitely a certain shift of consciousness that I like to think of as 'using the right-hand side of the brain'. It happens when we – consciously or unconsciously – stop trying to work something out in detail and fretting how we're going to do it and instead set our creativity free to find its own way.

More of this later, but for now I'd like you to think of an occasion when something creative you did just seemed to happen all of its own accord without much pushing or pulling from you. Can you recall how it felt as though you were suddenly in another dimension, where whatever it was you were doing – thinking, painting or exercising, for example – had a momentum all of its own? It felt wonderful, didn't it? And the good news is that whatever it is in our brain that facilitates this extraordinary shift into creative flow can be nurtured so that we use it to help us more and more often. Again, we'll be looking at this in more depth later on.

The inspiration for creativity is often referred to as our **muse** – we talk of 'finding and following our muse'. Think about that for a moment… Isn't it inspiring just thinking about it? The thought that there is a muse… or several… just waiting there for you – astonishing! But a word of warning – please don't be like the people who spend months or even years looking for a muse that sings out to them and bids them follow, and while waiting let their creativity lie fallow. You needn't look and wait in vain even for a day or two. When you free your creativity, it will, aided and abetted by you, find any number of muses all around you, ready and waiting to give you that special tingle of inspiration and, taking your hand, lead you forward along the oh-so-exciting and fulfilling path of creative flow.

One source of inspiration, for instance, can be consciously or unconsciously discovered in **our senses**. Think about yours – how do they inspire you? Perhaps you may find – or have already found – that sound is the muse that sparks your creativity and helps it flow. I often paint with some music playing in the background – or, depending on my mood and the nature of the painting, even with the sound turned up loud. The music seems to feed my inspiration and heighten the whole experience. Or sometimes I'll hear a piece of music, a wonderful lyric or melody, and it will fill me with a wild kind of excitement that makes me long to – and decide to – do something creative. Looking at art that moves me can have the same effect.

Inspiration could come through any of your senses – what you see, hear, touch or feel, or it could be a particular scent or taste. The possibilities are endless. At this stage, just keep in mind what has that inspirational excitement for you – we'll look at this again later and see how you can bring it into your life more and appreciate it to the full when it arrives.

Our various **everyday activities** can also be a rich source of inspiration. One of the most creative people I know looks to the company of people who uplift his spirits to inspire him, while another walks in the hills alone. Inspiration can come when we are caring for others or when we are working, whatever the nature of the work. These are just examples – there are so many pastimes and aspects of life that can give us the creative spark. Have fun noticing what does it for you and your own pattern of following it through.

The sixth sense, **intuition**, can give us creative guidance, too. It's a kind of knowing or understanding that can come from deep within ourselves or from another dimension, very often arriving suddenly as though out of nowhere in moments of quiet contemplation and reflection. Giving yourself the space to receive its message is something you can learn and is useful in many areas of life, but especially in showing us opportunities for creativity. Try connecting with your intuition right now:

Try this

1 Find a quiet oasis where you can take a few minutes to yourself.
2 Close your eyes and breathe slowly and deeply.
3 Relax all your muscles. Feel your shoulders, especially, drop, and any tension around your mouth or eyes dissolving peacefully.
4 Now start a sentence: 'Creatively, I'd like to…'
5 Let your thoughts drift…

6 Notice what comes into your mind – it might be one idea; it might be a string of them.

7 Focus on it – or, if there are several ideas, the one you want to focus on.

8 Feel if your body is responding physically – there might, for example, be a feeling of warmth between your shoulder blades, or what feels like a flow of energy running down your body.

9 Enjoy the inspiration and your physical and/or emotional response.

10 Come back into the everyday world.

11 Say thank you to your muse of intuition.

12 Write down whatever it is you'd like do creatively. This is very important – we always think we'll remember but so often don't – so a quick note will help it stick in your memory and jolt you into doing it.

Note! As a prelude to listening to your intuition, if you wish, you can – in addition to the second and third steps of the exercise above – use any other meditation technique you like (or try a favourite meditation/visualization of mine that may suit you, too – see Chapter 9.)

I did this for a moment as I started to write the above instructions and immediately what came to mind was 'Paint!' First of all, I thought, 'But I have been painting!' – but it took only another instant for me to know what was meant. I've been working on a series of illustrations for a friend's book of rhymes. For me, illustration, much as I love it, is organized work, whereas my painting is wild and playful. So at that moment of letting my intuition come through, I knew my heart's desire was to get my oils out and have fun with colour, letting my creativity flow unrestrained onto the canvas!

Another time it might be 'Cook something new!' or 'Walk by the sea!' A neighbour the other day received the message to spend time tinkering with his beloved but neglected vintage car. And one client with whom I did this meditation told me: 'I had the strong idea that we [her partner and her] need to think sideways and be creative about ways forward for us.' They'd got stuck in an endless cycle of repeating the same thoughts about their relationship and whether or not to stay together. She was right – creative thinking can be a boon in changing a couple's negative pattern. She remembered the intuitive wisdom that came to her, and with her partner she came up with a new path that enabled them to continue to live together but be happy in their individual lives as well as in their togetherness.

This may sound like a digression but it's valuable because it shows how creativity and intuition can breathe life, energy and renewed positivity into all sorts of aspects of our lives, relationships included. Certainly, they need to go hand in hand with love – and creativity and intuition naturally do just that, loving us and wanting the best for us. And so intuition can gives us exactly the right inspiration for the moment and situation we're in, highlighting an idea or vivid image perhaps, or pointing out a previously unconsidered possibility for handling a delicate situation, or finding a solution to something.

Like so many elements of creativity, intuition is an instinct we all have but which many of us use rarely, if at all. With encouragement and practice you can bring intuition back into your life and benefit tremendously from its help in all aspects of your creativity.

Whenever you are doing something creative, try letting your intuition guide you. Be intrigued by the way it takes you and enjoy the way it illuminates your path.

Another valuable source of creative inspiration is **training and learning**. Whether tutored or self-taught, as we learn we develop our brainpower and various abilities, including our creativity, which thrives on fresh thinking. Whenever I go on a course, even if the subject isn't (you would think) anything to do with creativity, my creativity is re-energized and becomes eager to leap forward. The course doesn't even have to be brilliantly taught or particularly interesting (though, of course, it's even better when it is) – the challenge and novelty of doing something different is all it takes to shake and rattle our creative brain cells. So I highly recommend a learning curve – it will give you the zest for living creatively.

Experience and practice are such a mine of creativity! The better we learn to do something and the more we practise, the more easily our creativity springs into life and flows. Doing something well – even the simplest or, some would think, boring occupation – is potentially a fount of inspiration. As a temp, years ago when I left school and didn't know which direction I wanted to go in, I did several repetitive jobs that didn't require a lot of thought or present much of a challenge, but I found I loved the way I could soon learn to do them well and then get better. My school years were spent at a highly academic school where I often struggled unconsciously with the teaching style. As an adult, it gave me a welcome feeling of accomplishment and purpose to find myself not just coping well with a real, working life, but thoroughly enjoying it and being appreciated and praised. An even greater bonus was that it somehow enabled my previously squashed creativity to start to grow and blossom in all sorts of ways. It took many more years for me to unlock my creativity as a painter – but that's another story...

Suffice it to say that I will pass on all the keys I've discovered – my own and other people's secrets, too – that will make your creative journey equally joyous as my own, but, I hope, much easier.

The spiritual realm is the numinous source of creativity into which we can tap. One of the forms of intelligence we are born with is the ability to connect spiritually and metaphysically with the dimension beyond our current understanding of the world and universe we know. I call this the 'seventh sense'. Artists of all kinds have often spoken of the inspiration they've received from times of connection when, through their spirituality, they have somehow made contact with a greater intelligence or a form of energy that spoke directly to their soul. And as viewers of paintings or other visual artwork, readers of poems and other literature, listeners of music, and so on, we too may have a sense of connection with the ineffable mystery – a sense of goodness, light and love that transcends this life and energizes our own creativity.

Give yourself every chance you can to connect with your spirituality, for it is not only inspiring but *healing*. It always feels good and it can be joyous. One way is to give yourself space for contemplation or simply the silence that allows you to sense the sacred. When you feel this connection, cherish it. It will spark and nurture your creativity and give to your creative work a rare quality of spirituality that others may tune into.

Insight

Enjoy looking at the sources of creativity and see how they can give you new inspiration and also feed your existing flow of creativity. Any one of them may hold a key to unlock your creativity or any aspect of it that's blocked or as yet untried. Looking afresh at something, noticing its impact on your senses and allowing yourself to feel it to the full is a great way to get in touch with your creativity and let it flow. Which of the sources speaks to you now, at this very moment? Take advantage of the help it's offering. Go for it!

Contacts to fire your creativity

We've mentioned learning as a source of creativity – now let's look at ways it can stream it into your life. It's very individual – we all learn in our own way and at our own pace. Think of the people who have best taught you – the **teachers** who made it easy for you to absorb information and whose love of their subject inspired you. Make a list of them and give them thanks in your mind – or for real if they're still around! They won't just have been school or further-education teachers and tutors; you'll have had others in your life who have inspired you and taught you all kinds of things.

You may have been lucky enough to have had **mentors**, too – people who encouraged and inspired you and made you feel *able* by holding out their frame of knowledge, expertise, experience and contacts for you to climb. All through your life keep looking out for people who teach you things or in other ways inspire you to learn. As you increase your knowledge and wisdom, you'll nurture your creativity at the same time, because creativity draws inspiration from all kinds of things and the more you know, the more there is to draw upon.

Seek out the ideas and thoughts, the wisdom and creativity, of others: your friends, your colleagues and your family, strangers with whom you just happen to have the chance to talk. Each one is a fount of learning in their own individual mix. Any one of them may provide inspiration for you in some way. A lot of it is about having a positive attitude – people who listen to your thoughts, encourage ideas and are rarely critical or dampen your spirits are inspiration and creativity angels. Sharing love, hope and joy give us the feel-good factor, lifts our creative souls and lets our spirits dance.

The company of people who make you feel good can fire your creativity, too. You know that feeling when you seem to be weightless – whether quietly enjoying their presence alongside you or chatting away nineteen to the dozen? Think how good it feels and how it seems to make your soul rejoice. Reach out for more of that conviviality and give it generously, too. Your ideas will spark ideas in them and vice versa. At work, even people who normally like to work alone occasionally or often find that teamwork adds extra zest to their creativity.

Right through my life I've found a succession of **gurus** of various sorts who have helped me realize or remember my inner creativity and spurred me on to free and have fun with it. It started with my father, a schoolteacher gifted with both imagination and practical skills so that he could, for example, turn our 2D pictures into 3D models. An early fan of J. R. R. Tolkien's *The Hobbit* and *The Lord of the Rings*, he built a wonderful model of the Shire and Mordor for his class. I was also greatly inspired by C. S. Lewis and *The Chronicles of Narnia*. Even today, if I need to shake up my imagination and faith in myself and my creativity, I'll walk through real or imaginary pine trees, in my mind entering Narnia – metaphorically another world where anything is possible.

Think of the people, books and films that have fired your imagination and creativity. Put them into print or pictures and they'll be an easy instant way to go to that place of creativity in your timeline and be inspired all over again whenever you need a fix of motivation.

As well as being a *result* of our creativity, **rewards** are another valuable *source*. Above all, the emotional fulfilment and buzz of being creative keeps our creative energy springing, and is a great incentive for continuing to think and live creatively. Selling our work, peer recognition and wider celebrity can also be satisfying, not just on the financial front but in boosting our confidence and inspiring more creative endeavour – but they're the icing on the cake and not at all essential to the joy and deeply satisfying fulfilment of creativity.

Probably the most reliable source of inspiration and creativity is **habit**. Shine the light on your creativity every day, live and think and breathe creatively, and you'll forge a wonderful way of being. The more creative you are, the more easily your creativity will flow. Being a living thing, the flow of ideas and output will vary – but when they're a daily practice, they'll always be there for you. Show up for them, too!

Who is creative?

You are! We all are. It's a myth that only evidently arty people such as visual artists, musicians, writers, film directors, and so on are creative. In our everyday life we demonstrate our creativity pretty much continuously and with a lot more scope than previous generations – we have so many modern gadgets and so much technology at our disposal with which to exercise all the various kinds of creativity. And with other gadgets to help with life's work and chores, we have more leisure time available to us, too. Start to recognize when you're being creative and be aware of the thrill it gives you. It might be anything from a stirring of interest, a small or large charge of pleasure to a real shot of excitement – just notice it and enjoy. It's like stroking your creativity ability and saying thank you to it. You know how good it is to be welcomed, encouraged and praised? Your creativity loves all that, too. So appreciating and relishing it this way doesn't just care for it but positively encourages it to develop and thrive.

Do you need talent to be creative?

Initially? No – not a scrap. Ability? Yes – absolutely. But we all have ability in various creative ways. By beginning to use it, or using it more, and learning and taking inspiration from the many sources we've talked about, you can grow your ability and may well find an aptitude for some seriously enhanced creativity that you would never have dreamed you had. Here, in your own hands, you'll have discovered you do have talent.

When I think of the stores and reserves of hidden creativity humanity must unknowingly harbour both in terms of ability and potential talent, it blows me away. Just think – in unlocking yours you are not just opening yourself to creative fulfilment and happiness; you are contributing to the world's flow of creativity, of which we need every quantum particle to protect and help our world survive and flourish.

Opening up your creativity

We've seen how most aspects of our lives and nearly every activity can demonstrate our creativity and/or be the launch pad for it.

The master key to recognizing your own creativity and connecting with this ever-present creative energy is to live *mindfully*. It's so easy in today's busy world to zoom from one thing to another or multitask so much that we find ourselves doing everything on autopilot without thinking about or appreciating what we're doing. Your creative spark, in this kind of frenetic lifestyle, may struggle to emerge and you probably won't have the chance to even be aware of it.

If you recognize yourself in this picture, organize your life so that you can slow down. Surprisingly, it doesn't take much. As I thought about this, I realized that I was rushing, typing as fast as I could. And in that instant I breathed deeply, slowed down, found my shoulders and back relaxing – and remembered to enjoy the moment. All it takes to recognize the creativity within and all around us is to be mindful, just for a few moments:

Try this
1 Stop rushing around or worrying about all kinds of things.
2 Breathe slowly and deeply.
3 Relax any muscles that are tensed, especially those shoulder and neck ones, your upper arms and the ones around your eyes.
4 Be aware of your self – your soul and your creative spirit in this moment.
5 Breathe! Feel how your breath fills your lungs and leaves them again.
6 Breathe in peace, have confidence in your ability to do what needs to be done at a steady pace, quietly and competently.
7 Breathe out negativity and stress and rush.
8 Know that your creativity is here for you now and is always available to you. It is part of you – inspiring, imaginative, sideways thinking, problem-solving.
9 Love it. Give thanks to it and for it.
10 Come back into the room, feeling calmer and energized.
11 Smile – you are a wonderful, thoughtful, creative person!

Throughout the book, we'll be looking at all the kinds of creativity, but most of all seeing how life – *your* life – can be beguilingly, satisfyingly creative. All the keys you need are available to you. Setting free your own individual creative elements is going to be fun.

6 POINTS OF REFLECTION

1   A little time daydreaming and using your imagination will encourage your creativity to come out and play.

2   Every time you use your ingenuity and are resourceful, you are being creative. Use your brain – it's a great gift and works in tandem with your creativity.

3   Remembering the various ways in which you are particularly creative will remind you of your astonishingly wide scope and ability.

4   Notice the sources of creative inspiration that work for you. Return to them whenever you need refreshing and a helping hand.

5   Be aware of people whose company and teaching has inspired you in the past or resonates with your creativity today. Even the thought of them is manna for your inspiration and creative flow.

6   When you're being creative, or want to be, pause for a while to focus and let the inspiration come through and flow.

2

Practical ways to get in touch
with your creativity

In this chapter you will learn:
- *how your creativity can light up your life and the lives of others
  and play its part in the wellbeing of the world, too*
- *how to introduce a creative approach into everyday writing to
  let creativity flow*
- *other ways to spark your creativity and keep it vibrant*
- *how to live creatively.*

Letting in the light of creativity

We've seen the many ways your creativity may show itself in your
life. It's a part of you that is expressly designed for you. Its purpose
is to enhance your life, opening you up to an ongoing sense of
curiosity and adventure, an excitement and fascination about this
extraordinary world we live in and your particular place in the great
scheme of things, and also to help you cope with the whole process
of living.

Think, for a few moments, about your astonishing potential to live
in a way that is an asset – a living, breathing help and joy – to our
wonderful world. Every one of us has the ability to make a difference
to our own and others' lives, and to our planet both locally and
globally. Instead of feeling hopeless and helpless to contribute, take
a few seconds to pause and feel the thrill of beginning to recognize
your creative power. Working hand in hand with your innate ability,
it's there to enable you to thrive and fulfil your potential in all sorts
of ways.

Scientists, artists, mathematicians, teachers, medics, parents and carers, manual workers, craftspeople, entrepreneurs, retired people and those who don't work or who haven't yet found their metier... every single walk of life offers all kinds of possibilities and paths where creativity is not just a valuable personal asset giving contentment, happiness and fulfilment but is itself the key to unlocking better ways of doing things that will benefit others.

This applies to all manner of creative solutions, and segues through all the various technical, emotional, spiritual and environmental aspects of life. As we can each make a beneficial difference to our own and others' lives by living creatively, just think of the immense energy for good we harbour at our ready disposal if we all raise the bar on the extent to which we are creative.

One of the most illuminating and transformative kinds of creativity, though often unrecognized as such, is problem-solving and troubleshooting. Although we can all recognize problems, often, swamped by them, we sink into anxiety or inertia. But recognizing a problem – whether it's personal or a global one – is the point of entry to solving it, and the more creatively we think and live, the sooner and the more competently we will find answers.

Similarly, in difficult situations, especially areas of conflict, an openness to creative thinking enables us to use our senses and abilities holistically to find a way through the maze of objections, claims and viewpoints as well as rights, needs and wishes. When we open our minds to think creatively, the application of common sense, hand in hand with kindness and compassion, is more powerful than the most complex computer and the light they let in enables you to go to the heart of the solution.

In any problematic or complex situation...

- ▶ listen to all the viewpoints
- ▶ look at all the implications
- ▶ don't feel you have to 'fix it' immediately
- ▶ be prepared to live inside the problem for a while, taking time to feel its various nuances and letting your mind and creativity work together to understand its dynamics
- ▶ above all, keep calm – you help no one when you are agitated
- ▶ don't make the mistake of thinking yourself inadequate for the task – you are more able than you know

- ▶ be open to letting your ability and creative power flow through the complexity of the situation to explore, heal and seek solutions
- ▶ now and then meditate, quietly ponder, be still and be aware – listening and keeping all your antenna alert for ideas and perhaps a revelatory vision.

Insight may come fast or it may take time – be patient but at the same time be ready to act when the time is right.

How to introduce a creative approach into your everyday life

As catalytic as sunshine on flowers, awareness of your possibilities is all it takes to trigger your creativity, while attention and gladness enable it to blossom. In all probability, as you're reading this book, you'll be aware you're creative, even if it's just a gut feeling you've rather neglected or for some reason thought you should deny. Or perhaps you didn't think you were creative but would like to be. Now it's time to recognize the potential scope of your creativity, take it in your hands and decide and pledge to appreciate and encourage it.

Start each day by...

- ▶ taking a look at the list you made (in Chapter 1) and remembering how creative you are in all kinds of ways
- ▶ being ready and open to express your creativity
- ▶ sensing the feeling of warmth and anticipation this gives you
- ▶ writing your 'start-the-day pages' – see below.

Knowing how creative you are – and you are, very much so! – and taking any of the steps suggested in this book, will have a direct effect on your brain. Just as the innate creative gene can be recognized in children and their ability expanded and honed, so you can start caring for yours at any stage of life, including the present. The more you do creatively, the more you will want to do and the more able you'll become. It's a kind of intelligence that, like any other, improves with learning, practice and perseverance and, especially, with enthusiasm.

If ever you falter in your faith in your creativity, do the following exercise to remind yourself of your ability.

Try this

1 Take a large sheet of paper.
2 Jot down, off the top of your head, one or two ways you're creative in each of the following:
   ▷ *at work* – e. g. thinking of the best way to do a task, encouraging others, daydreaming!
   ▷ *in your home* – e. g. choosing colours, cleaning efficiently, cooking
   ▷ *playing with* or *teaching your children or pets* (if you have them) – e. g. suggesting games that are fun, learning with them, planning walks
   ▷ *in your hobbies and leisure activities* – e. g. being imaginative, building a team, generating ideas, making something
   ▷ *in your relationships* or *friendships* – e. g. giving surprise gifts, thinking of loving gestures, phoning spontaneously.
3 Now write in BIG LETTERS: 'YES – I REALLY AM CREATIVE!' and glow in the knowledge that you are.

A big part of introducing yourself to the truth that you are a highly creative person is remembering that, while you didn't learn the full extent of your creativity at school for whatever reason, you have the rest of your life to foster it, make use of it and, above all, enjoy it.

Forget the myth that only a few people are creative. We all are, as we've already discussed. Sadly, there's a common tendency to relate creativity to wealth and celebrity – but such instances are largely dependent on determination and/or luck and fashion. Most of us aren't creative in particularly notable or fashionable ways, perhaps aren't good at marketing, or perhaps are simply the world's quiet souls who are happy being inconspicuously creative. But everyone *is* creative and *can* shine creatively, even if their glow is generally unobserved in the privacy of their life.

It's normal, however creative we are, to occasionally doubt our ability. It can follow harsh criticism, or be a response to something physical like low blood sugar. Suddenly, we'll think 'Perhaps I'm not as creative as I think and it's all a mirage!' When talking with others about this, I've discovered it's something we all feel now and then. The key to not abandoning or locking up your creativity in these circumstances is to do any of the creative awareness and self-confidence exercises in this book and soothe the irrational fear by reminding yourself that, actually, yes, you are creative – genetically in the first instance and now increasingly because you're nurturing your creativity and enjoying experiencing it develop.

However, one word of caution. Please don't expect to be instantly good at something. For instance, if you want to express your creativity as a painter, don't feel you have to be a great painter immediately and sell paintings within weeks. For every prodigy there are a million slow learners and burners. It doesn't mean your creativity isn't there, or won't develop – it is and it will. Make your mantra: 'Enjoy the *process* and don't get hooked on *product*.' We'll look at this hugely important point further throughout this book.

Free-flow writing as a daily conduit for your creativity

I was introduced to morning writing many years ago and it's been a boon and a joy ever since. Everyone to whom I've recommended it swears by it, too. It's a catalyst for creativity – sparking it and keeping it flowing right through the day.

There are three main forms:

1 Totally free-flow, random writing where you have no guidelines whatsoever and just let your unconscious take you where it will via your pen.
2 A journal – much like a diary in that you catch up with the day before, but rather than being controlled, instead, you let your unconscious fill in whatever details it likes and go off at any tangents it wishes to.
3 Thoughts on anything that's on your mind or perhaps something interesting that's come out of a dream or thoughts triggered by the day ahead.

Depending on your personality, you can choose which form of writing is your favourite. Being an incorrigible Gemini, I like them all – so my favourite thing is to see which I fall into when my pen hits the paper and quite often I'll find myself flowing from one to the other in the same session.

Here's how to go about it:

> **Try this**
> ▶ Have a pad of A4 paper by your bed so that all you have to do is reach out for it first thing, as soon as you wake up.
> ▶ Start writing and keep going, non-stop, until you've filled three sheets of A4 paper.
> ▶ Write whatever comes to your hand, letting your hand move across the page as fast as it wishes.
> ▶ Single words. Phrases. Sentences. Paragraphs. Continuous text. All are fine, in any combination.
> ▶ Don't worry about grammar, spelling, content or style – all you have to do is let words flow as they will. It doesn't matter if it's complete gobbledegook – the point is to let words flow on to the paper. Just keep your pen moving across the page.
> ▶ Don't stop – keep your hand moving until the whole page is covered and then another and then another.

Three pages, for some reason, seems the perfect length, no matter what the size of your handwriting. Probably it takes the first to get into the process and relax; the second to continue the flow and, as in jogging or other aerobic exercise, find your second wind; and the third to enjoy the feeling of writing in flow as you head towards the end of the session.

You may find, at first, that the gobbledegook lasts for all three pages, and even into the next day or two. Don't worry – that's fine. Sooner or later words that make some kind of sense will start to flow. Both before and as they flow, don't monitor them or try to guide them – let them do their own thing.

You'll find that, once this practice becomes familiar to you, after a few lines of nonsensical writing thoughts start to flow onto the paper. Sometimes it's all pretty prosaic and on other days something really original and creative may come through your writing. However, it will always have a positive effect on your creativity generally, even though this may not be apparent at the time. It's as though it loosens you up and let's creativity flow in all sorts of ways throughout the day.

It also provides a rich resource to look back on. Even years later I'll sometimes look through an old free-flow notebook and find something inspiring or thought-provoking I didn't notice before or much enjoy revisiting. Where I wrote about everyday events, it's so spontaneous and full of sensuous impressions that it's extremely emotive and transports me instantly back to that time and place. It might remind me of the emotional place I was in at that time and throw an interesting light on how I've progressed – or not as the case may be! Or perhaps I'll come across something surprisingly lyrical that will give me an idea or set me off on some fresh piece of creative writing. Many's the poem I've discovered in or between the lines of thoughts that long ago tumbled onto the paper. So it's important to keep everything you write, as it can be such a creative treasure trove.

To avoid any feelings of self-consciousness or the need to edit as you write, remember that this writing practice is totally private and won't be shown to anyone. It's just for you and your creative flow.

Apart from being a wonderful way to unleash a flow of creativity, it's a lovely way to start the day. It's simultaneously calming and energizing, person-centred and affirming, so, not surprisingly, whenever you do it, it will feel good and be a great springboard into the rhythm of the day.

Curiously, despite all these benefits, you may find you have a resistance to actually doing it! This is most likely due to fear that you won't be able to squeeze out one word, let alone three A4 pages. Don't fret – you will – put your pen on the paper and it will get going, despite your mindset!

The point of doing it as soon as you wake up is that this is when you're naturally close to your subconscious. You haven't spoken to anyone, listened to the radio, put your mind to the day ahead, so your subconscious is free to flow onto the pages any way it wishes.

But if you're decidedly not a morning person and are truly uncomfortable with the thought of doing it, then set aside a space later in the day; the first-thing-in-the-morning requirement isn't set in stone, although it is a great way to start the day if you can muster the resolve to do it.

Must you do it *every* day? Although I highly recommend it, there's no *must* about it – it's your choice completely. However I would suggest you do it most days because it's so valuable in sparking and enriching creativity. And it is an absolutely essential exercise whenever we feel our creativity is being held back or is even completely blocked. It's as useful as that well-known multi-purpose lubricant that you spray on anything that's gone rusty to free it up: it soothes, smoothes and seemingly magically gets everything working again. Practised pretty regularly, it frees up your creativity in all kinds of ways and keeps it flowing. And, like any beneficial practice, the more regularly we do it the easier and more pleasurable it becomes.

It's a good idea, too, to have a place where you can store your free-flow writing – it makes it special to you – which, of course, it is.

Insight

A4 is the ideal size of paper for free-flow writing as it's big enough to accommodate a lot of words, however large your writing, and to let the momentum gather pace as you swing across the page. And, yes, it does need to be in your handwriting as it simply doesn't work so well with keyboard and screen or by using a voice recorder. There is something about the direct contact of the pen in your hand that lets the words flow from your subconscious.

Try it for yourself, practise it and persevere – and, above all, enjoy it!

Remember – it's all *about* you and it's *for* you.

More ways to spark your creativity and keep it vibrant

Life is such an astonishingly complex wonderland of opportunity for being creative and throughout the book we'll be looking at potential sources and muses. As a starting point, along with free-flow pages, the following strategies will inspire your creativity every day:

▶ **Day boards** allow you to stick or pin up anything that interests or appeals to you and are treasure troves of inspiration, comfort and pleasure for creative people of any age. They're wonderful for storing mementos that will instantly excite your creative taste buds. Pictures you've clipped from newspapers or magazines because they in some way make your heart leap; quotes that inspire you or make you think sideways; photos you love; poems that speak to you; paintings you resonate with – all these can be the starting point for a creative journey or an inspiration along the way.

▶ **Scrapbooks, notebooks and sketch pads** are also useful for storing all kinds of thoughts that occur to you through the day, interesting things people say and all kinds of little snapshots of life. Again they're a valuable resource that, both in adding to them and revisiting them, can often provide a trigger for something creative. The more pictures there are, the more appealing they will be and the more you'll enjoy looking through them. Sketches (and you don't have to be Leonardo – naive is fine and will make you smile, too) are great to look back on and, like certain phrases and sentences in your free-flow pages, will take you back mind, body and soul to the moment you made them. It's very personal, very original – in short, a very creative and a welcome resource whenever you need a little bit of pure delight.

They will become steadfast features of your creative life. However, I'd also like you to add the following as essentials, too: play and gurus.

PLAY

Play is to creativity what salt is to our food – it enlivens, refreshes and in a way brings to life its essence. Above all, playing is fun and makes us laugh – a sure and quick way to get our serotonin and other feel-good chemicals surging and, in the process, renew our optimism, self-confidence and stream of ideas.

I have a young dog whose *joie de vivre* is intoxicating and catching. When she was a puppy I sometimes, at first, found it frustrating to have to keep stopping work to take her out. However, I quickly realized, that, because she saw every outing as an opportunity for fun, it got me on side and did me – whatever work I was absorbed in – the power of good. Soon she no longer had to ask me to play with her – it was me who would suggest a quick game whenever my progress slowed or even when I was in full flow. Now we play anything from football to 'round-the-house it'. My neighbours probably think I've regressed to childhood. But perhaps that's what it's all about.

You don't have to have a pet or child to play and exercise with, though it does help! Any kind of play where you get puffed out – dancing, for example – and laugh out loud, and perhaps get excited in some way, too – as in many kinds of sport – is excellent. And if you have got fellow humans around, enjoying conversation, joshing, challenging each other's perceptions in debate – all these are another kind of play that can energize and uplift you.

However you like to play, you'll get those energy-making chemicals flowing and give your creativity a great boost, too. Aim for some play every day. Laughter and engagement are a true tonic for creativity.

GURUS

Gurus – the popular word for inspirational teachers who use their particular knowledge and wisdom to guide others and lead them a stage further forward in their lives – are also a tremendous help in increasing and recharging our creative energy levels. The sign of a good one is when you feel they are speaking directly to you and are on the same wavelength creatively, personally and perhaps spiritually, too. You like them tremendously and feel they would like you, too, if they only knew you.

Find yours by keeping your eyes and ears open. You might, for instance, read a review of a book that compels you to read it, or an interview that makes you think that this is an interesting person who can teach you something or whose philosophy will take yours a stage further.

That, really, is what a guru is all about – taking you a stage further. Unlike mentors, you may never know them personally, but they will nevertheless be a blessed guide through their books or perhaps through a lecture, workshop or seminar they're giving.

However, if you're fortunate, you may find a teacher running classes near enough for you to learn from them in person. Gurus can help you in your particular specialism or any subject in which you have an interest, but they are most associated with a deep spiritual and philosophical wisdom that illuminates creativity generally.

Over the years I've had several gurus. It's an enriching experience and feels as though your hand is metaphorically being held warmly as they lead you forwards in understanding and inspire you to deepen your understanding and creative ability. With the right guru, you absorb information and understanding quickly and with less effort than you would with a teacher with whom you don't have this special kind of empathy. It almost feels like learning in another dimension and/or a form of osmosis – as though molecules of knowledge are transferred from mind to mind (and perhaps they are!).

Sometimes we learn from a guru throughout our lifetime, continuing to benefit from their influence long after they've died. Sometimes we learn all we can from them and move on, remembering with warmth and gratitude the help they gave us but ready to be taken forward by another teacher. It's said that the next guru comes to us when we are ready, and that has certainly been my experience in matters of philosophy, spirituality, art and, one of my particular interests, natural horsemanship.

Gurus truly do change our lives, helping us to mature as people as we learn and develop, and also helping us to expand and develop our creativity. Look out for the teachers who are special to you in that that they have a quality that seems to speak directly to your soul as well as teaching you in a very practical way. They are treasures of your life. Work with them, and always, of course, do your very best. They are a gift to you and your creativity, and they will help you to shine.

How to live creatively

Living creatively involves using our minds creatively, with our brains working in close co-operation with all our senses.

THE ART OF LISTENING CREATIVELY

That's really listening – not just hearing what's being said, but taking it in, paying attention and thinking about it, with care both for the person and what they're saying.

If you're listening to music, either enjoy it or turn it off. There's no place in creativity for mindless background noise that doesn't please you – it tires the brain and dulls your sense of hearing. Music you adore is amazing. Engage with it and it lights up your whole being. It's emotive, sensuously enlivening and sets your creativity alight.

By tuning in to the sound all around you can also tune into your creativity. Try this exercise:

Try this
1 Sit quietly.
2 Breathe steadily slowly.
3 Relax any tensed muscles.
4 Become aware of all the sounds you can hear.
5 Be patient, taking in the various different ones.
6 Appreciate the different levels and tones, the intricacies and textures.

26

7 Think how else you would describe each sound you hear.
8 Can you feel your creativity 'humming'? If so, luxuriate in the feeling. If not, imagine you can and imagine luxuriating in the feeling.
9 Live with your sound 'picture' for a minute or two. How does it feel? What is your main impression of it?
10 Enjoy the realization that you've just been listening creatively.

Carrying this exercise out myself, just after writing this, I can hear the computer humming, a clock ticking – and then, as I listen more attentively, layer after layer of sound behind the first sound emerges – the buzz of some machine (the fridge probably) in another room and, in treble tones that seem to sit on top of everything else, birdsong. Then I notice the tapping of my fingertips on the keyboard, and the sound I make as I swallow and touch my teeth together. Most of this I am normally unaware of, and it makes me think how I could use it if I were writing a novel, or simply as a useful part of the relaxing and overall awareness process if I were settling down to meditate. The process of tuning into awareness of the sounds of the moment makes me feel peaceful and focused.

THE ART OF LOOKING AND SEEING

The two people I know well who look and see most comprehensively and clearly would both claim that they're not creative. But they are, and particularly in this ability and skill. Steve is a joy to explore a place with because he notices so much – be it in the country or the town – but it was during a tour of the Rockies that I realized how superbly refined is his ability to see what there is to be seen. It was as though he could look through undergrowth or trees, or deep into a river or pool, and see what was apparently invisible to everyone else – myself included until he'd point it out to me. We saw all sorts of 'critters' including bears, beavers and eagles that were hidden from most people's vision. His knack and skill is born of loving life and using the gift of sight to pay attention and register everything it shows him. I've got better at looking since he taught me the importance of these basics but I have to work at it after years of *not* looking.

Then there's Walter who has spent a lifetime immersed in the countryside and, like Steve, has an acute ability to see thoroughly and in acute detail. Over and over, he'll notice things I miss, however much

I think I'm improving! But his particular skill is to take in *how* things are – how nature is coping with weather conditions, for instance, and how people are – *really* are – even if they're not intending to express these things.

Good ways to use your gift of sight creatively are to...

▶ look through the layers of the scene before you. By that I mean, as well as noticing the foreground, you look *through* it to what's next, and next and next and on into the distance. Sometimes you'll find it's as though you have to 'tune in to' or 'get an eye for' things you wouldn't normally have noticed at all.

▶ Feel your brain working as it takes in all the things you can see and appreciates their diversity.

> Try this
> **Next time you're by a river, pond, lake or harbour, look at the water.** At first, you'll probably notice what's on the surface – reflections, ripples, water beetles and so on. Now look down into the water, adjusting your eyes, and, if you have them, donning a pair anti-glare sunglasses. Take in what you're now seeing, down beyond the surface and on through the different levels.
>
> Notice how you're feeling. What impression are the various things – the colours, life, movement, etc. – that you can see making on your emotions and your other senses?
>
> Have fun thinking how you would represent the things you see if you were going to paint a picture of them. You don't have to actually do this – though, of course, you can if you wish – but just visualize the picture you would like to paint, the colours you would use, whether you'd add words, the kind of style you'd adopt.

THE SENSES OF SMELL, TASTE AND TOUCH

These all impact on our creativity, too. So don't ignore, neglect or otherwise belittle them. Appreciate them, noticing them so they can be an important individual part of your consciousness and aid your overall awareness, too. So often I'll hear someone say, 'Oh, I haven't got a very good sense of smell,' and that may be true in that it's not strong, but it doesn't mean it's not sensitive. Start – or, if you already do this, practise it more – making a point of using your sense of smell. Smell the scent of something right now. For example, hold your forearm up to your nose and drink in the scent of your skin – both the scent, and how you receive it, is unique to you. Think how you would describe it if you were writing a love letter to yourself. Appreciate the wholesomeness of it. Love it. In so doing, you will love yourself – your being, your life.

Similarly, when you taste something, appreciate to the full the sensation it gives you and notice any effect this has on your thoughts and other senses. How would you describe a particular taste if you were, for instance, a passionate television chef, expressing your enthusiasm, knowledge of your subject and individual perception?

Think how you would describe the sensation of touch – what it feels like both to touch someone else's skin and to be touched by someone else, for instance. Or how it feels to stroke a cat. Immediately, the awareness of other senses kicks in. Thinking – not quite laterally or sideways but through the dimensions of our senses like this – is an extraordinary exercise in our creative being.

As I mentioned in Chapter 1, the sixth and seventh senses are also important to our creativity. We'll look at these in more detail in Chapter 9, but for the moment be ready to be intuitive, and to connect with the sacred beyond our world.

Be ready to think both literally and laterally. Think, think, think! You have an extraordinary brain and use only a minute portion of its ability. Start using it more! Try taking new approaches, have a creative and positive attitude, love with all your heart your work, your play, your dear ones.

By opening up your being this way, you unblock all the channels and let creativity flow.

Insight

Life – every day of it – is a new creation. Think of it as a blank sheet ready for as much creative action as you wish to muster. Creativity hums through all our lives – from the quietest to the busiest. You are at the heart of your being, your life, your creativity. Live it and love it with zest.

6 POINTS OF REFLECTION

1 Don't underestimate your power to make the world a better place. By living creatively and using your mind and abilities well, you can be a good influence on any situation in which you find yourself and those around you and this can radiate out further than you'll ever know.

2 Every day be aware of your creative possibilities and potential and you'll be ready to step into them.

3 Listen, look and use all your senses. They are the allies of your creativity.

4 Do some free-flow writing every day. It frees up your creativity – pure and simple – and once it becomes a habit it's easy and feels good.

5 Remember to play and have fun – you and your creativity may get jaded if you don't. It's good for your soul, too.

6 Be alert to inspirations around you and keep an eye open, always, for anyone who may be your next teacher.

3

Encouragement

In this chapter you will learn:
- *how to adopt, develop and nurture self-belief*
- *the power of focus, thought... and then relaxation*
- *how to be your own biggest ally and advocate*
- *to set yourself challenges*
- *to choose your critics with care.*

Appreciation and encouragement

Creativity responds positively to our attention and particularly thrives when we encourage it with appreciation and enthusiasm. Like self-confidence, it doesn't take much non-constructive criticism for our creativity to dive under cover and there stay dormant for the rest of our lives if we don't invite it to join us again. Fortunately, creativity doesn't sulk unless *we* do, and the moment we acknowledge it and offer it the chance to express itself, it will be raring to go again.

I stopped painting and drawing when I was eight after my art teacher roared with laughter at one of my drawings and let the whole class join her. I took it as a verdict that I was rubbish at art. Although I'd been doing well, I hadn't grown enough self-confidence to survive the knock and didn't pick up a brush or crayon again until one day years later as an adult I was so inspired by spring colours I just simply couldn't resist. I still have the little paintings I did then and love them for their joyful quality. But those around me teased me and once again I gave up. But luckily, encouraged by Maggie, an artist friend, some years later again, I had another go at painting and loved it so much I vowed I would appreciate my creativity and be loyal to it for ever more, no matter what anyone said! Her encouragement invited me to paint again, but the difference this time was that I'd become much more confident and knew I was creative in all sorts of ways and I was happy to express it to the full in my painting, too, whether or not anyone else rated my output.

Since then both the process of painting and the pictures I've made have been a huge delight to me. It's an extra bit of bliss when someone else resonates to my work, but it's not necessary to my enjoyment of it and any negative comments slide off me now. So don't be super-sensitive. You don't have to wait for years to let your creativity in any particular area flow. Go for it now and enjoy it to the full, no matter what anyone else says about it.

It's especially important to encourage any new creative output you have, whatever the area. Fledgling creativity is as fragile as any new-born living thing. Of course, our first efforts probably aren't the greatest; we're beginners and we will learn and progress in time the more knowledgeable and experienced we become. So it's not silly or arrogant to be enchanted by your early work. Pride in it is manna to your creativity and absolutely justified because, whatever the quality in your own or other's eyes, it is a genuine expression of your creativity.

And don't be deterred by teachers or well-meaning accomplished friends who try to teach you too much too soon. Look for the ones who see the good in what you've done and praise it – and you – and realize that you will learn or absorb knowledge and experience as time, and practice, continue. You don't need to rush.

Most of us learn best by encouragement, praise and very gentle, step-by-step teaching. All of these nurture our creativity and keep our spirits both intact and high.

Give yourself and your creativity lots of tender loving care by...

- ▶ using your creativity in whatever way you wish to express it
- ▶ having the confidence that what you create will be as good as you can do at this time, and realizing and being glad that that is very good in its own unique way
- ▶ enjoying the satisfaction of having been creative
- ▶ praising yourself – I often say to myself 'Good girl, Jen – well done!' at the end of the day.

Creativity doesn't have to come in long stretches of time. You might, for instance, be creative all through a two-hour stint of making something, or it could be a flash of inspiration, or a moment when you have the nous and kindness to say the right thing to someone. However you've been creative, be aware of it and thankful. Your creativity will thank you for the appreciation and be automatically encouraged to return next day. The more we accept encouragement and praise, the more creative we become – it's part of the momentum and flow and it feels good.

Treasure any creative buddies you have. My sister, the writer and artist Penny Stanway, is as entranced with the joy of creativity as I am and we're thrilled by each other's work and love to encourage each other and, whenever we get the chance, enjoy the fun and inspiration of painting together. My artist and writer friends all inspire me hugely, too – my heartfelt thanks and love to you all.

Insight

So often people have a go at something creative like writing or painting and give up when their early work isn't applauded and/or they don't sell it. Use your creativity because you simply love being creative. Enjoy the process and the flow and encourage yourself every step of the way. Give thanks for your creative ability, however naive or clumsy. And don't daunt yourself by thinking about the amount of work it will take for your work to become 'good' in the eyes of the cognoscenti. Everything creative you do is 'good' if you do it with love and enthusiasm – it is good for the stage you're at and a testament to your creativity. Enjoy!

Self-belief – how to adopt, develop and nurture it

We flourish when we believe in ourselves and when others believe in us. And our intelligence in its many forms, including creativity, is largely dependent on our own conviction, too. If we think we're good at something or can become so, then we probably are or will be. When we believe in ourselves it's extraordinary how much becomes possible.

Because creativity is sensitive, we need to notice it, pay attention to it, love it and care for it. Today, instead of being self-deprecating either in your mind or out loud when you're talking with others, stand up for your creative intelligence. You know when you have an aptitude for something. Instead of hiding it, be open and glad about it, for its light will light up your life and others'.

It helps to understand why we put ourselves down. Most of the time, when we deny or play down something we're good at, it's either because we fear sounding arrogant or because we think others will envy our ability and therefore like us less. Actually most of us love it when others are positive and shine with confidence. It's infectious – because their light shines on us, we automatically feel good, too. Yes, a few people may be envious – however, it's not your diffidence and reticence that will help them overcome this but your happiness in your creativity and encouragement of them to use theirs.

Creativity is all about originality, new life, growth and development. Given free rein, it is naturally exuberant and abundant. In full flow, it has astounding energy and is continually replenishing. Never ever squash it – instead, delight in it and know that it is yours for ever – a miraculous asset totally individual to you.

Insight

Think for a moment of those whose creativity sparkles in their comedic talent. The funniest aren't those who determinedly hold centre stage but those who draw others into their circle of laughter by encouraging and appreciating their active response, funny thoughts, experiences and jokes, too. Again, the joy is palpable and hugely infectious – laughter is all the more fun when we're generous with it. It's the same with all kinds of creativity – being generous to ourselves and with others lets it sparkle.

Undo any damage already done to your creativity by your own or others' scepticism, and free it to grow afresh, vigorously and 100-per-cent positively, by reprogramming your belief in it and your ability to let it flow. It isn't a case of pretending or in any way deceiving anyone; it's simply creating a picture of how you sense deep down you can be – creative, original and talented in your own particular way.

Visualization and **affirmation** are very powerful tools psychologically because they allow us to step into or reclaim our given creative territory. You were born with your own mix of creativity – instead of suppressing it, speak up for it! With such a marvellous innate ability, it's entirely natural and good to not just want to use it to the full but to enjoy and delight in being supportive of it.

34

Maximize your creativity with this exercise in belief that your creativity can flow as you wish it to:

> Try this
> 1 Sit quietly, breathe deeply and slowly and relax all your muscles.
> 2 Be aware that this meditation is for your benefit and for the joy it brings in releasing your creativity.
> 3 Think of a way in which you would love your natural creativity to flourish (e.g. having good ideas; in one of your hobbies; in your work).
> 4 Imagine a situation where you are using your creativity in the way you'd like to.
> 5 Now step into this picture and take in the detail. See where you are and how you're being creative.
> 6 How does it feel? What do you especially like about it?
> 7 How do you see this situation developing? What would you like to happen?
> 8 Imagine following this path as your creativity enhances your life.
> 9 Understand deeply and surely that you can free your creativity to benefit your life in just this way.
> 10 Give thanks for your creativity and affirm that you are letting it flood your life with all the help and pleasure it is meant to give you.
> 11 Give it permission to find the best ways of bringing about the way you wish to use your creativity.
> 12 Now gently and quietly step back into your daily life, knowing that your mind has taken full note of the scenario you have envisaged and will work towards bringing it about.

The last two points are extremely pertinent to our creativity. When we visualize a situation and imagine living within it, we effectively introduce it to our mind and our creativity. They take it on board and explore it and, as long as it's going to be good for us (it wouldn't work if it wasn't), they get a feel for it and naturally do their best to bring it about.

How this happens we don't know, but it's astonishingly effective. When any aspects of a visualization or detailed daydream are unclear or for some reason not possible, our mind will improvise and do its best in the circumstances it's been given to work with. So it's very important to visualize in detail and be sure to include anything you see as necessary to the whole picture. It's also essential, of course, that you are realistic. What you are doing is asking and freeing your mind to use your creative ability as you've visualized, but this must be in accordance with your ability. In other words, it isn't miracle working – it's simply harnessing all your mind's power and energy to bring about the situation you would like to be in.

The power of focus, thought… and then relaxation

Just as we aim for the goal on the football pitch, or our own personal target in all sorts of sports, so having a goal on the creative front is a powerful and extremely effective incentive. Yes, there's probably groundwork to be done first to hone our ability to reach the target, but even when we have the necessary ability, it won't get us there if we don't believe in it. To demonstrate this, try this simple physical test to see how far you can jump along a path:

1 Mark a starting place.
2 Stand there and without further ado jump as far as you can.
3 Mark where you landed and mark a place three inches beyond it.
4 Now go back to the start and look at the furthest mark.
5 Still focusing on it, and aiming right at it, jump again.

You will almost certainly have jumped further than your first jump and, if you didn't quite reach the target, you soon will with focus, determination and practice. It's the same with everything we do, not just physical things. If we focus on where we want to get to and aim for that goal, we will do better and better until, as long as it's realistic, we achieve it. Golfers, billiard players and other sportspeople are taught to 'see' the result they want for each stroke or move they make – their coaches understand that, with this in their mind's eye, they will encourage themselves to give it their best shot and step into that very picture. It's just the same with creative ideas. Imagine clearly – really live it – the creativity you want to experience using and enjoying, and by doing so, you will invite it into your life and encourage yourself to do whatever's necessary – spotting opportunities, practising, persisting, etc. – to make it become your reality.

There's nothing new about the technique of visualizing where we want to go, whether it's a simple next step or a complete situation. It's been given all sorts of names – for instance, 'mind pictures'. For it to work, it's important to remember two keys:

1　You need to remember to practise it – this seems so obvious and yet, like so many good habits, it's easy to forget.
2　You need to do it in your best interest. That means for whatever is right for your mind, body and soul. If you use it for financial greed or to be in some way superior to others, it won't work. Using your creativity with a good intention, on the other hand, is positive and loving and encourages your whole being to move towards it.

Another way to use the power of focus is to have periods of intense thought when you explore every aspect of a creative question you're asking yourself or the plan you want to progress. Really focus on it, bringing all the power of your conscious brain to take it in and consider it fully. Then leave it be for a while and think about other things, do something else, or sleep. As you let go of the question, you'll experience a lovely feeling that you've done all you can and a sense that your subconscious can now take over without you having to tax yourself any further. When you let your mind have free rein like this, it will use its incredibly sophisticated powers to explore holistically all the aspects, nuances and possibilities of the situation, and finally present the solution.

Although I've stressed the importance of detail, it does help if you are prepared to compromise. Sometimes we can't have it all, or have exactly what we want, but our subconscious will come up with something similar and good for us in its own way. For instance, if you are an actor, you might visualize playing the lead in a production. However, you might simply not be right for it in some way, or not right in the eyes of the producer, but nonetheless find yourself having a lot of fun without all the pressure in a different part or perhaps in a non-acting role.

To date, despite the exponential advances in technology, we have yet to come up with a computer that comes anywhere near the complexity and vibrancy of the human brain. When we're conscious, we use only a small fraction of our intelligence and capacity –

but when we free it and ask it to help us it will do so, often subconsciously as we are relaxing, concentrating on other things or sleeping. Perhaps it will do so by working with the information it already has stored and bringing the full extent of our intelligence to it. Perhaps it will suggest to you that there is further research to be done to provide the knowledge it needs to help. And perhaps it will draw on the sixth and seventh senses of intuition and spirituality… but more on those later in the book. What matters is that our creativity will be greatly enhanced and our ideas and wishes given a big helping hand when we free our mind to search, unencumbered, for creative solutions.

I stress again that it may not come instantly. Often, certainly, an answer or response to a simple question or problem will be with us within a day or two. But in complex situations involving other people with several sets of wishes and needs overlapping, it may take much longer. I will often wake up in the morning and find that the idea or creative solution I've been looking for pops into my mind. On the art front, I may 'see' the picture I want to paint and all I have to do is get the brushes out and start painting. The first line – or sometimes the whole – of a poem I've had a vague idea about may present itself fully formed. Or perhaps a good way of resolving a social dilemma will suddenly become clear.

For creative help with the various major life changes I've faced – for instance, moving to a new area or changing career direction – it has usually taken longer. Again, in such complex circumstances, I needed to explore them fully and do everything I could to consciously help myself. Then I could set my mind free and humbly ask it to come up with a solution or resolution that was viable and attractive. For me, there is also a big spiritual element here – I believe that, when we ask for help this way, we somehow draw down and/or invite help from a spiritual element. Again, more on this later. However it comes about, a way forward will come to us in time. Perseverance in believing that it will and patience are the keys.

Develop the seven principles of creativity

People who are clearly recognizable as being creative often have seven main things in common. All of these are encouraging and positive and you can make all of them your own. Like these people:

1 believe you are creative
2 believe in your ability to let your creativity flow and benefit you
3 constantly or at least regularly put your creativity into practice
4 keep learning and improving
5 be open to new ideas
6 value others' creativity
7 constantly encourage yourself by generously appreciating your creativity and having faith in it.

Be your biggest ally and advocate

While it's lovely when anyone admires something we've made or said, we don't have to rely on others' approval – we can give our creativity all the encouragement it needs ourselves.

If ever I'm feeling a bit dull on the creative front, or even completely stalled, I'll use a mixture of cajoling and encouragement to re-energize my creative spirit, for instance by saying to myself: 'Come on – you know you'll love it once you get going, and as soon as you do, you'll pick up momentum again.'

I will also pick one or more of the thoughts and exercises in this book and use them. The ones I most often use are these:

▶ Free-flow writing – if I'm sluggish, it's a given that I haven't been doing this lately.
▶ Meditation.
▶ Doing something – anything! – creative (see the next section).
▶ Picking up a book that may help and opening it. Somehow – like always finding a new, appropriate teacher just when we're ready for them – we will be attracted to a book that gives us just the inspiration and encouragement we need at that particular time.
▶ Remembering that the word 'encouragement' means giving courage. Be brave and take a first step – that's all it takes to get going again.
▶ Thinking of yourself as your own ally and advocate – this way you will naturally be on guard against sabotaging yourself with negative thoughts and criticism and you will be good to yourself.

- Imagining you are teaching a child or a good friend: you will be then as inspirational, encouraging and kind as possible, won't you? You will be careful not to dash their spirits by taking them too fast too soon and expecting too much of them. You will appreciate the value of making it a good experience for them with praise and encouragement. You will have strong faith in their ability, however currently un-honed. From now on treat yourself just the same – with love, goodwill, patience and faith in your ability. Doesn't it feel good just to think this is how you will behave towards yourself? Do it!

Take one step…

The easiest way of all to kick-start our creativity is to decide to take one small step.

I'm sure we all have 'if only' thoughts: 'If only I had a room of my own', 'If only I wasn't married', 'If only I had more money', 'If only I'd had parents who'd encouraged me'… Well, yes – it would be nice to have more space, time, money, mentoring and so on, but actually these are all extraneous to our creativity, so refuse to use them as an excuse not to be creative.

You can be creative all through the day in all sorts of ways, wherever you are, however you were brought up and however busy your life is. And by taking one small step you will not only put paid to the 'if only' scaremonger, but you will step over the initial fear of starting.

As an artist, for instance, you might tell yourself you can't work because **you don't have enough space**. For the time being, then, take the step of picking up a sketchpad and making a sketch – of anything. Encourage yourself by remembering that you don't need a lot of time – even a two-minute quick sketch will make you feel good because you'll have done something creative and realize that now you can go on from there – practising – looking – seeing – sketching – loving that thing you're drawing with all your heart and mind and endeavouring to catch the essence of it, however simply.

As an ideas person, you might say **you haven't time** to put them on paper. But in any spare moments you can let them come into your head and jot them down in a notebook. That's all it takes to start. Just a word or two if you're in a rush will be all it takes to be able to revisit them and work them up later.

Not enough money? Few earn their living expressly from their creativity and most of us have other work. But we can still be creative in all sorts of ways that don't require a big spend. And we can always take some of our leisure time and set it aside for focused creative activity if we need and want to. If you are serious about your creativity and want to express it, you can – step by step.

Regret you lacked **parenting or mentoring** that encouraged your creativity? As above, helpful though that would have been, it's not essential because you – as we will see over and over throughout this book – are from now on going to encourage yourself and act as your own ally, advocate and mentor!

While it's good to look at the whole scenario when we're making mind pictures of living our creative dream, when you long to do something creative but feel helpless or thwarted, it's often because we're looking at the big picture and are overwhelmed. Forget the big picture of producing an astonishing body of work and instead do what you can do now – take the small step that you do feel able to achieve in the right direction. If you're a writer, it could be a paragraph of your novel. An artist, a quick sketch. An inventor, a thought or question. A thinker, take ten minutes to put your mind to a philosophical question. And so on and so on – however you wish to express your creativity... one small step. It will free your mind and your creativity to do more.

Once you've taken one step, the next will be easier and so on, exponentially, until you are creative every day as a matter of course.

Take that first step. It's a matter of life – your life, your creativity, your joy.

Creativity loves a challenge

The self-set challenges that are so helpful in instigating and progressing any creative process may be anything from a small promise of a reward to a major throwing down of the gauntlet.

In everyday creative work, I often bribe myself with a promise of reward, too – for instance, I'll say 'Get such and such done and you can have a cup of coffee.' It sounds simplistic, but do try it with a reward that appeals to you – it works! Creative spirit is like a child in that it loves small rewards that it can win easily – and when we've taken that small step and gone the distance set it isn't just the coffee that's the reward, it's also the sense of satisfaction and pride that comes with it, plus the feeling that, now you've completed that leg of the path, you can get on with the next stage refreshed and with renewed enthusiasm.

CASE STUDY

A big challenge might have a huge impact not just on our creativity but the course of our whole life. George, a successful professional artist, worked for years at another career feeling increasingly frustrated because he longed to devote his working life to his passion for painting. It was only when his sister-in-law said to him, 'You'll never be much good at it – why not be satisfied with doing a bit of painting at the weekend?' that he finally resolved to do something about it.

'Her patronising attitude infuriated me,' George told me, 'and I decided there and then that I would show her and the rest of the family that I did have creative talent.' Having saved enough to take a sabbatical from his job, he painted and painted until he found his style and a genre that pleased himself and the market. 'I would never have had the courage,' he said, 'if she hadn't said that. It was a challenge I had to rise to – and I did.'

Understanding and defusing subjective criticism

Just like George, we can turn subjective criticism to our advantage. Almost everyone who is creative, whether an artist of some kind or a creative thinker, finds themselves criticized at some point. This may, of course, be fully objective and justified and then, when it's put to us kindly and sensitively, you'll be glad to have the critic's assistance in improving your work or line of thought – a good, constructive critic is your ally.

But creative people often find their work the target of harsh criticism that's subjective. It could be that the critic doesn't understand it, simply because it's different and they've never come across anything like it before and this makes them feel hostile. Or perhaps something about it reminds them of a personal past experience and they transfer their emotions from that onto your work. There are also critics who derive a sense of power and superiority from belittling others' efforts. Sadly, there are those who are jealous of others' creativity and only too ready to sabotage it. Or it may simply be that it's not to their taste and they can't get beyond that.

Being the butt of subjective criticism could all too easily wound your creative spirit and so it's vital to be able to put up a shield to deflect it. First of all, try this exercise as it's helpful in understanding just how subjective criticism can be, so that you can guard against it. And besides, it's great fun to do!

Try this
1 Choose a well-known abstract or Impressionist painting by a painter who is now revered.
2 Imagine you are a critic seeing the picture for the first time and for some reason or other you take against it and loathe it.
3 Write a description of the painting in this vein, detailing what you think is wrong with it.
4 Sum up your personal feeling about it – how you feel and why.
5 Then see the same painting through different eyes.
6 Imagine instead that you are a critic who resonates with the painting and falls in love with it.
7 Write a description of the painting in this vein, detailing what you think is right with it.
8 Sum up your personal feeling about it – how you feel and why you love it.

I much enjoyed doing this with one of Vincent Van Gogh's sunflower paintings. Negative criticisms included: childish, clumsy; garish colours; bad drawing; a disaster.

Positive criticisms were: joyously naive; colours that sing; a keen understanding of botany that makes the flowers so lifelike you can smell them. Stunningly beautiful. Gosh, the man could paint! A masterpiece!

Van Gogh, of course, sold only one picture in his lifetime but today is revered as one of the finest artists of all time.

Whenever you need encouragement to weather adverse comments, take a moment to reflect on how subjective criticism can be. Remind yourself, on receiving criticism, to assess whether it's subjective or objective. If the former, refuse to be defeated by it. If the latter, consider it thoughtfully and use it constructively.

Either way, you can use it as a challenge to spur you on to more creativity, and to strengthen your self-belief. You know you are creative. No one else can ever take that away from you or diminish it in any way...

- ▶ Believe in yourself and your creativity.
- ▶ Be glad for it.
- ▶ Give thanks for it.
- ▶ Laugh – while it's good to have faith in our creativity, it's not good to get too 'up ourselves' about it! Laughter is a joy and gets everything back in perspective.

Remember that, in the absence of encouragement from others, we can give *ourselves* bucket-loads of encouragement.

And always remember to encourage others' in their creativity, too, and, of course, not to be negatively critical. Only give an opinion if it's positive and encouraging, and only criticize if asked to. What goes around, comes around. Besides – enthusiasm feels as good in the giving as in the receiving.

6 POINTS OF REFLECTION

1 Appreciate your creativity and wealth of abilities and talk to yourself encouragingly when you wake up and throughout the day. Be a good friend to yourself.

2 Value yourself highly. Yes, of course you can do more and be more – we all can. But each day, this is where you start the rest of your life and giving grateful thanks for your being is a great start. Be a staunch ally of your self-esteem and your confidence will grow strong.

3 Work enthusiastically and do the best you can. Then relax to replenish your physical and creative energy.

4 Everything creative starts with one step forward. Take that step!

5 Choose your teachers and appraisers with care – ones who will encourage and inspire you.

6 Accept their challenges if you believe they're appropriate for you and your creativity, and set yourself challenges along the way – small or large, they help you to keep stepping out.

4

A creative attitude

In this chapter you will learn to:
- *think more creatively*
- *play creatively*
- *enjoy the creative power of curiosity*
- *appreciate the wonder and mystery of the world*
- *thoroughly enjoy being creative.*

What do *you* think about things?

We're naturally thoughtful. As very young children, we think about everything because everything is new to us and we need to take it in, roll it around in our minds, and absorb our sense of it. Our brains are active all the time we're awake – and probably processing it all as we sleep. We use everything we learn creatively in our play and daydreams.

As we grow older, however, gradually our leisure time is increasingly guided by others and daydreaming is often discouraged, or perhaps there's just no time for it as life becomes cluttered with extracurricular activities, homework and social life. At school and in higher education, we are taught what others have previously learned and thought and we have to keep up with the latest research and information, too.

So we learn to concentrate on taking in others' discoveries, their inventions, their philosophy, their wisdom. We need this base of knowledge to pass exams and also to give us a sound foundation in life. However, it worries me that teachers and tutors are now so pressured to make sure the curriculum is fully met that they often have no time or motivation to inspire their pupils to think originally for themselves. With luck, there are debating societies where pupils are encouraged to think and express their views, but even so it's very possible to go right through the education system without having the chance, let alone being encouraged, to think originally.

This kind of information channelling even happens at art schools and on adult education courses, where students learn to consider their own ideas in the context of earlier or contemporary art, and to practise copying it. So even when students do think for themselves, their work is often similar to what's gone before or to what happens to be fashionable now.

After years of absorbing others' thoughts and achievements, it takes courage and zest to appreciate our freedom and do our own thing. Many have already become complacent – they don't need to think, so why bother? Others are very comfortable living in the light of what has gone before. This is all very well, but it's so much better when we bring our own light and spirit to our creativity.

When you want to live a creatively vibrant, fulfilling life, the first essential is to practise thinking your own original, independent, new, fresh thoughts! Your mind is unique and you have ample capacity to think for yourself. Whether you use the material you've digested over the years to nourish your own creative, personal line of thought or come up with completely new ideas and concepts, be sure to think and feel and love what you're doing. Use your mind to look at life from different angles with an open mind and ponder:

▶ Can it be done a different way?
▶ Is there another solution?
▶ Am I missing something?
▶ Is there another way of looking at this?
▶ How would I have approached this if I didn't know how others have?

A highly creative graphic designer, Philip, laughed one afternoon as he told me how he had been struggling with the best way to position his new sofa. It had seemed clear that there were two possible places for it and he couldn't decide which would be best. Suddenly, he told me, he'd had a 'light bulb' moment and realized that there was actually *another* ideal position for it in the room. By mulling the question over, he'd suddenly opened himself up to an option that hadn't previously been obvious at all.

This kind of willingness to let new ideas come through – whether they appear from your subconscious or the ether – stands us in good stead in all aspects of life from everyday issues such as interior design to potentially great artistic, scientific, business and philosophical breakthroughs. Picasso and Einstein had a good foundation of learning but they let their creativity flow, too. However unlikely we are to come up with amazing work like theirs, we can all let our creativity flow through our lives. It will enrich your spirit and give you joy in the newness and wonder of life and your part in it. You and your creativity are valuable in your own way and have something to give to the world. Thought is as precious, as life-giving to your creative ability as oxygen is to the body.

Get the knack of creative thinking by giving yourself **time to think**. It could be while you're doing something else if you like to multi-task: at the gym, for instance, you can be thinking as you work out. Walking, swimming and other solitary sports are great activities for thinking. When you're driving, or as a train, plane or bus passenger, use the time to think.

And develop your thinking by **discussing** it. If they didn't grow up in a home where everyone talked and chewed things over, and they didn't go to a school which encouraged debate either, people can be frightened of expressing their opinions. If this applies to you, don't worry – you can get used to expressing your ideas but you'll need to go gently with yourself as you begin to do so. Like most new habits, it takes time to practise and become comfortable and confident with it.

Email correspondence is another great platform for exchanging views, too. I have two email buddies with whom I 'talk' about everything and anything. They put me right when my thinking's off course and reading their views helps me get mine in perspective, too, and often teaches me something new. Social websites and blogs can be useful in the same way.

Thought and debate are naturally inspiring and, as well as being a form of creativity in their own right, they are particularly conducive to other forms of creativity. You'll often find that, if you have a session of deep thought or a buzzy conversation that has made you think, you'll suddenly feel an urge to do something else creative – making something, for instance, or expressing your creativity at work in any manner of ways.

Developing a creative attitude

Picture your creativity like a ball of clay that's just right to work with:

- ▶ It has a lovely texture that's malleable yet firm.
- ▶ It's sensitive to your touch and wishes.
- ▶ It will hold its shape when you want it to.
- ▶ It's deliciously sensual.
- ▶ It gives you a feeling of possibility.
- ▶ It hums with purpose.

In short, it invites you to use it, love it and make something of it. Every day, every moment, your creativity is at your disposal because you are a creative person.

Think how you love it when you've done something creative: it could, for instance, be that you've had an original thought or idea, or a great conversation where you've used your mind to follow or guide the line of thought and really enjoyed it, or perhaps you've made something. However you've been creative – and remember there are any number of ways you may have been – it will have given you a good, uplifting feeling.

It's a feeling you can recapture any time you like by choosing a creative attitude. You know that feeling when you're a bit jaded, flat, dissatisfied or grumpy for no apparent reason? And/or you feel tired, again for no physical reason? Explore the mood, and almost certainly one of the reasons – perhaps the sole one – for it will be that you're not using your creativity.

When we go for a certain length of time without using our creativity we feel out of sorts because it's such an important part of us. How long we can be uncreative without feeling the pain depends on individual personality and how practised we are in our creativity. For someone who's rarely creative, it may have become pretty much a way of life to feel you're missing something. It's like a dull ache – a longing. If you are very creative and reading this to help you let your creative energy flow more easily and/or more often, you may find that even a day with no creative expression is uncomfortable for you.

Just as we have a deep need to connect with others, to be aware of our spirituality, to look after our physical wellbeing, so we need to take notice of our creativity and let it flow.

Free your creativity by paying it attention. Heed your creative need, first of all by reviewing your creative output recently, and then by aiming to let it flow again:

Try this
▶ Think of the last five times you did something creative. (Refer back to Chapter 1 and your list of the ways you are creative to help you consider this.)
▶ Relive how good each experience of being creative felt.
▶ How long have you gone without doing something creative?
▶ How long have you gone without doing something creative especially for yourself?

Now:
▶ Ask yourself what would you love to do now on the creative front?
▶ Let your mind go blank and listen for an idea to sing to you. It will!
▶ Think what it will take to follow this creative impulse and make any plans you need to be able to put it into action.
▶ Beware of 'buts' – we all have a negative side that comes up with obstacles – instead choose to be completely positive and say: 'Yes, I'm going to do it.'

It's astonishing what a constructive effect this simple exercise has on mood. Thinking 'How can I be creative? What would I like to do to express my creativity?' makes us instantly feel better. Even the thought – which, of course, is intrinsically creative – triggers an increased flow of serotonin and other feel-good chemicals. And once you start actually being creative the way you're subconscious has urged you to be, you feel more and more energized.

However happy we are in other ways, however good our lives are, being creative enhances it. However miserable and however bad our lives are, being creative alleviates the distress. Creativity is manna for the soul and makes life better – and you'll find that, as you pay attention to it, use it and love it on a daily basis, it will becomes easier and easier.

So instead of ignoring your creative need, or suppressing it by engaging with so many other activities that you don't have time to think of it, or trying to drown it with alcohol or other drugs, listen to its message of longing and hope and embrace your creativity as a part of your everyday life. Notice and feel the way it's there for you in so many aspects of everyday life. Dip in and out of this book whenever you need to be reminded or want some inspiration. Talk to other like-minded people who love being creative and share the joy of it. Most of all, remember that you are very, very creative, relish the knowledge, give thanks, and use it!

Insight

Attitude has a huge effect on our creativity: negativity tends to make creative ability go into hiding but, by taking a positive, loving attitude to your creative ability and energy, you automatically let it flow. It's revitalizing and feels great.

Playing creatively

What with being creative, thinking, working, family life, housekeeping, hobbies, socializing – we want to have it all! And not surprisingly life today not only takes a lot of managing but a great deal of energy, too. What saves it from becoming a relentless grind is a sense of humour, plenty of love, of course, and a liberal sprinkling (or indeed dowsing!) of fun.

We've already looked at how exercise, laughter and playing are great creative energizers, helping to take away any angst and lightening us up.

Insight

Passion is wonderful and vital for many forms of creativity – but we need to look after it with care or it can wear us out. However passionate we are about our creativity – and this applies to even, and perhaps especially, the greatest artists and other leaders in all fields, we need to maintain a touch of levity.

Yes, we need to take our creativity seriously – but too serious a take on it, too much of the time, sabotages its inherent joy and we can all too easily descend into anxiety and depression. We need to be aware of this danger and, if we start to feel anxious, take steps to relax and consciously protect and nurture ourselves.

Play and joy and love of oneself as well as others all help reset perspective, tempering the highs and lows of creative success and keeping us on an even creative keel. Once again, it helps to remember the games we played as kids – this time the ones that made us think and be sassy. Many card games, for example, require one or the other or a mixture of ingenuity, imagination, logic and resourcefulness as well as physical co-ordination. I especially loved board games where I could use my imagination and my favourites proved useful in adult life: Monopoly developed a passion in me for making houses into homes and an abiding fascination with the property market; Cluedo taught me to use my mind in a different way, reading the signs and looking for information and that's still useful in any research I do today; and a great game about horses that my father made for my sister and me complemented my girlhood love of them and helped fuel a passion that is as vibrant as ever today and which has taken me in all kinds of directions. All games that make us think, use our minds and encourage our imagination, too, are creativity at play.

Try this
▶ Think of the games *you* loved as a child.
▶ How did they encourage your imagination and ingenuity?
▶ In what ways has that been useful to you as an adult?

Now I'd like you to think of the games you play today – or, if you don't, ones that appeal to you. Again, card games can be a great fun way of exercising our creativity – think of whist, bridge, cheat, liar dice and poker! Board games like Scrabble are wonderful for our minds generally and very creative. And so in a sense are general-knowledge games because, in order to access the stored information in our brains, we need to practise being open to our 'mental search' results in much the same way as we have to be when we're 'listening' for creative ideas and guidance.

Go on – next time you're staying in for the evening, instead of switching the television on or reading, challenge your partner or a friend to a game. The connection, camaraderie and fun you'll share are all great for your creativity and wonderfully relaxing and the perfect antidote to any artistic angst!

Enjoying the creative power of curiosity

'Curiouser and curiouser,' said Alice as she explored Wonderland – and I'm pretty certain that her creator, Lewis Carroll, had inextinguishable curiosity about the extraordinary world we live in as well as the parallel one he conjured up so amazingly vividly. We wouldn't all hit the jackpot with a bestseller, but we could all enjoy conjuring up other worlds populated with scenery, places and beings unlike any we've seen here.

Try letting your mind run riot as you create your own imaginary country – it's good practice for your creativity and great fun, too. It could be entirely in your mind, or you could use a computer software program if you wish, or do it from scratch in words, illustrations or other materials. Have fun. Enjoy. It's totally yours to make and fashion and, importantly, love – for it's in loving your heroes and heroines and the beings who befriend them that you'll make it sing and dance with life.

In life generally, embrace the natural curiosity you had as a child. Ask questions of yourself and others all the time. I've been stunned as a mature student how rarely anyone asks questions – you've guessed it, I'm always the one that does. It's as though the others are scared to, or perhaps have lost their enquiring nature. But you learn so much more when you do – and nearly always someone will come up to me afterwards and say: 'I'm really glad you asked that – it was interesting.'

So don't be frightened to be curious – too much curiosity may be dangerous for cats but it isn't for us. It's a vital part of creativity that invites us to be imaginative, find things out, and have a zest for our fascinating world.

Try this
▶ Today and every day, find out something you didn't know before.
▶ At the beginning of the day, think 'I wonder what I'll learn today' in order to open yourself to opportunities to exercise your curiosity.
▶ Be alert to things that interest you that you don't know much or anything about.
▶ When you notice something that excites your curiosity, think what you'd really like to know and what good question(s) you'd like to ask.
▶ Be creative in how you find answers. You could ask people who are likely to know the answers, for instance, visit the library (if you're not used to the system, librarians are experts at tracking down the information you want and only too willing to help

you in your quest), and of course Internet search engines are brilliant for research, too.

▶ At the end of the day, reflect on what you've learned.
▶ Be glad you exercised your curiosity and learned something – doesn't it feel good?
▶ Think how you can use it in other kinds of creativity.

Appreciating the wonder and mystery of the world

You only have to think of the extraordinary complexity of the world we live in to realize that there must be countless billions of potential new thoughts, discoveries, ideas and all manner of possibilities. The day when coming up with something new or a new approach to what already exists becomes impossible will never come as, like our universe, ideas are infinite.

When you consider this, it instantly puts paid to those nagging self-deprecating or creativity-bashing thoughts such as: 'Who am I to think I can come up with an original idea when I've no specific talent?' or 'It's all be done before – I've no chance of discovering something new.' The thought of how much more there is to come on the creative front from the smallest ideas to world-changing ones is mind-blowingly exciting. Let's ask instead: 'Who are we to think we can't be creative when opportunities are endless and we each only use a tiny fraction of our brainpower?'

If you are serious about developing your creativity, I'd like you to be aware every day of the great sea of creativity you are living in. It's all around you – feel it, watch out for glimpses, notice when you tap into the energy of creativity in any way. Be aware now – right this minute:

Try this
1 Be still.
2 Breathe deeply and slowly.
3 Be aware of your whole body.
4 Relax your muscles.
5 Ask yourself if you can feel the excitement of creativity.
6 Where is this registering physically?

As I write, I feel the excitement of the thought of the creativity in me and all around me, and in and around you as you read this. I breathe deeply, relax and feel a wave of energy around my spine and shoulders. It's like an expectancy, gladness and excitement all in one, palpably registering in my physical body in harmony with my mind.

As you practise being aware of your connection with your creativity like this, also practise taking it a step further by asking: 'Which direction will it take me in on my next day off?' As I ask myself this, with my first weekend to myself for some time just ahead of me, I realize that actually I don't want to veg out. Yes – a bit of rest and relaxation would be good – but I want to do something creative, too, probably painting and generally being open to ideas as I talk with friends or garden or walk.

What will *you* do? A rain check like this is a great way not just to plan being creative, but to generate some feel-good energy for it, too. Raring to go like this, we spring into creative action and, complemented by, say, a lie-in reading the papers or time chatting with friends and family, it makes for exhilaration *and* satisfaction.

Choosing a 'what's-right' mindset

Just as you can choose whether to take a positive or negative attitude, so you can choose to think of your creativity in terms of what's right about it instead of what's wrong. For instance:

▶ Instead of saying self-deprecatingly, 'I'm not creative,' say 'Actually I'm very creative.'
▶ Instead of saying, 'I'm not much good at [for instance] art' (something you enjoy or would like to), say something positive like 'I'm good at colours' or 'I enjoy drawing and I am improving.'
▶ Instead of saying, 'I'll never get far with writing songs,' say 'I know that if I'm prepared to practise and learn I can do well.'

That's not to say we should be delusional! We do need to be realistic both about where we are now and how far we could go, but nonetheless it's terribly important that you should nurture your creativity. That means giving it your full support, loving what ability you have, realistically evaluating the potential, and being prepared to exercise it.

Insight

No one is born successful. But we are all born with various abilities in various measures and we can each take our ability, use it, practise and develop it and make the very best we can of it. That includes creativity. In fact, it is *all* about creativity for in a sense we create our own prowess at anything.

But I don't want you get the idea that realising your creativity is about slog and hard work. I remember once a television chat show presenter saying to the writer of an excellent self-help book about maintaining love in relationships: 'That sounds like hard work!' And he replied: 'No – it's not about hard work – it's about love and a willingness to understand what makes for a good relationship and how to transform your relationship with that understanding.' It's just the same with unlocking your creativity, appreciating it and letting it flow through everything you do – none of that is hard work, it's about...

▶ **love** – of yourself, your creativity, your ability and your gift to the world (more on this last one later)
▶ **willingness** to understand that by paying attention to your creativity you can nurture and hone it
▶ **appreciation** of the wonderful qualities of being creative – including excitement, fulfilment, hope and joy.

Thoroughly enjoying being creative!

As well as taking time out to play and have fun as a foil for taking our creativity seriously, let's remember to enjoy creativity itself. A commentator on the radio spoke warmly of the late Seve Ballesteros and said how unusual he was in the cheerfulness that complemented his passion for golf and in the way he smiled a lot. He said it was really refreshing as sportspeople so rarely smile today. Isn't that sad? Wouldn't we love them to smile more and openly enjoy their passion for their sport? It's much the same with artists – the prevailing culture seems to have assumed that art and creativity are Very Serious Indeed and any sign that those participating in them might be, heaven forbid, enjoying themselves would be considered frivolous.

But the whole point, for most of us, of pursuing our creative interest and passion is that it feels like home to us. We long to be creative in our own way, however simple or grand that may be. Just as a golfer adores the game with all his or her heart, so we others who are creative, whether it's in sport, art or any other way, adore being creative. Why on earth wouldn't we want to express this love and happiness? When we do it, it lights up not only the whole creative process but our surrounding life, too. It reflects on our loved ones and our relationships with them. It feels good all round.

Enjoying life – including our creativity – is largely a case of taking a positive attitude to life and deciding to enjoy it as much as possible. Quite enough bad things in life happen to us – sorrow, trauma and pain – but that makes it all the more important to enjoy the good things whenever we have the chance – and that includes our creativity. Do the following thought exercise:

> **Try this**
> ▶ What are your favourite ways to be creative?
> ▶ How do you feel when you're practising them? (Think of each one in turn because the enjoyment may feel different from one to another.)
> ▶ How do you express your enjoyment?
> ▶ When you're enjoying one of your creative interests or passions, pay attention to this enjoyment.
> ▶ Feel it fully and appreciate it to the full, too.
> ▶ When you wake in the morning, remember how good it felt and look forward to expressing and enjoying your creativity in the coming day.

Once again I urge you to be glad for your creativity. It will help you, your creativity and others. So show your happiness and smile!

Insight
Creativity is a gift and it's up to you to unwrap it, open it and be joyfully thankful. Revel in it. Use it. Treasure it. Share it. Positivity is a choice you make each day and it's great for every aspect of your creativity. In a spirit of appreciation, self-encouragement and enthusiasm, you can enjoy your gift to the full.

6 POINTS OF REFLECTION

1 Make a point of thinking creatively. Consider problems, for instance, from an all-round perspective, or take a sideways look right into them.

2 Have a 'Yes can do!' attitude as you recognize your ability to do something and do it enthusiastically.

3 Be like Alice in Wonderland – curious and ready to see how curious everything is!

4 See the wonder and mystery of the world all around you in everyday life, far afield and beyond in the inestimable infinity of the universe.

5 Resist getting bogged down by thinking of all the things you *can't* do. Instead, reflect on whether you may be able to do something one day, with training, experience and practice, or what else you could do in the same field that is within your ability now.

6 Think of all the things that are good about your life and your creativity and enjoy them passionately.

5

....

Freeing yourself from the blocks and defences that sabotage your creativity

In this chapter you will learn to:
- *free the self-esteem your creativity needs to flourish*
- *manage the negative emotions to benefit your creativity, not impede it*
- *how being creative can heal or even pre-empt depression*
- *think sideways about your talents and ambitions*
- *let go of envy and resentment.*

Freeing the high self-esteem your creativity needs to flourish

Healthily high self-esteem is a great benefit to creativity. It's a strong, level foundation upon which we can be creative with confidence and enjoyment. However, as we go through life, we take a bashing from so many directions. We're criticized by others and we criticize ourselves. We make mistakes. We don't do as well as we thought we might. We sometimes get scared. Sometimes we're not very nice to other people. Sometimes they're not very nice to us. In so many ways, we learn that life isn't as easy for us as we thought it would be when we were children. Perhaps we're not as liked as we'd like to be. Perhaps we don't turn out such good work as we'd like to. Not surprisingly, swept along with the flow of all these negative assumptions and experiences, our idea of our worth often gets severely dented.

But the reasons for this diminishment of our self-esteem are too often distortions of the truth. All focus on the negative.

Positive thinking – and by that I mean a realistic, all-round perspective, or *constructive* thinking – will allow you to get to grips with the reasons for self-esteem that's lower than it should be, and to lead it back to the high level you deserve.

Do you deserve a high level of self-esteem? Absolutely, yes. How do I know? There are several reasons:

▶ You wouldn't be reading this book, let alone this section, if you didn't believe in yourself, your essential goodness and your creativity.
▶ You came into this world with a unique personality and mix of abilities including creativity. You clearly want to make the best of them. That's sensible and also very brave.
▶ Something inside you is telling you that you are an interesting, valuable person.
▶ Something inside you is rebelling against your not being appreciated fully.
▶ Something inside you wants you to think well of yourself.

And I know you can do it – you can start thinking well of yourself. It will work wonders for your creativity and your confidence both in your creativity and in yourself.

It starts here. This moment. Make a pledge, to yourself, that you will treasure yourself from now. You are treasurable – and you can decide to realize this. Always – whenever sabotaging thoughts arrive – remember it and, instead of being sucked into them, refuse, absolutely point blank refuse, to let them depress your self-esteem.

To help you whenever you're feeling sceptical about your merit, remind yourself of the things you like about yourself. Now and then make a list in your head, or make an actual, definitive list and keep it somewhere you can easily have a look at it whenever you need some reassurance.

Think, too, of ways that you *try* to do your best, even though you haven't succeeded as well as you'd like in accomplishing them. And every day remember that you can do your best to honour the person you are, your present ability and your potential.

The eighteenth-century German philosopher Immanuel Kant said there are three great life questions and I've added another:

1 What can I know?
2 What can I do? (This is my addition!)
3 What ought I to do?
4 What can I hope for?

These really say it all on the question of self-esteem and creativity because...

▶ you can truthfully recognize what you already know and can learn
▶ you can assess what you can do in any aspect of your life, including – and especially – your creativity
▶ you can, with thought, think what you ought to do for the good of yourself, your creativity, others and the planet
▶ *and* you know in your heart, and can also work out realistically, what you can hope to do.

Do all these things, with daily or at least frequent reviews to keep you on track, and you'll be leading a good life and caring positively for your creativity, too. Your self-esteem will blossom and so will your confidence.

And to make sure you keep them flourishing, a sensible move – though one we so often ignore – is to mix with people who make you feel good about yourself. That's not to say sycophantic people who suck up to you, but people who genuinely value you as you are and encourage you to be your real, best, creative, unique self and the way you want to be.

It's also important to avoid or minimize contact with anyone who undermines or openly attacks your self-esteem and creative flair. This could, of course, be difficult if someone you are bound to keep in your life, and/or whom you love, puts you and your creative endeavour down. It's astonishing how the nicest people can get in the habit of being insidiously mean to someone they really love. They may not even be aware they're being mean just because they've got so used to it. Or for some reason they may even *intend* to hurt you and/or sabotage you and your creativity. Or they may have the misguided belief they're being funny: 'Oh darling – you know I'm only *teasing*!'

ANY undermining is bad for your self-esteem and likely to be disastrous for your creativity. And so you must put a stop to it now and in future make it clear you won't tolerate it. It helps to explain that you find the digs and arrows hurtful and tiresome. Hopefully, once you've drawn their attention to it, they'll realize what they've been doing and stop it. But if they don't and they try it again, say no to it firmly and mean it.

It's astonishing and hugely liberating to realize that, once people realize you mean it, they nearly always stop. They will recognize your new confidence and self-respect and naturally respond by giving you respect, too.

Of course you may still receive undermining comments from others that catch you unawares. I keep a list of 'The Things People Say' and laugh over the extraordinary callousness or clumsy tactlessness of the comments with my good friends. It's a great morale-booster and it's fun.

You *are* a good person. You *are* creative. You *do* think well of yourself.

And I, for one, am cheering you on.

Managing negative emotions to benefit your creativity, not impede it

The way we can guide the emotions that affect our work was brought home to me in sharp relief recently. I went to see two art college graduate shows, both with excellent reputations. In one of the exhibitions the work through all media was almost universally colourful, bright and aesthetically beautiful. I was uplifted and, as I left the college, I felt as though I was walking on air full of hope and music.

At the next show it was very different. The work was mostly monotone; where it was representational, the subjects were tense, taut and often tortured, and where abstract, the same sentiments still came across strongly. I was equally moved, but this time to sorrow and deepened concern for humanity and our world. I preferred the first show, but that was purely subjective, and no doubt others would have favoured the second.

But the fascinating thing was that clearly each set of tutors had steered their students to use their emotions in a strikingly different way. This resonated personally with me as at art college as a mature student one of the tutors tried hard to get me to change from my beloved bright colours to monotone ones. 'Think dark, evil, black,' he said. 'Bring out the passion of your dark side and paint it!' Reader, I did it and I sometimes use the technique now – but, while it produces very different work, I habitually return to the bright colours and subject matter I love as they are natural to me and feel good.

However, it taught me something profound which was reaffirmed at the graduate shows: just as we can guide our emotions constructively to enhance our lives, so we can influence our creativity with them and use them to produce rich and sometimes powerful work.

Let's look at some negative emotions to see how, first of all, they can be managed constructively.

ANGER

Focus on this feeling and how it affects you physically – where does it manifest itself in your body? As you look at the causes – and there's often one or more underlying the presenting one – relax the muscles that are 'holding' the tension and let go of the destructive quality of the anger. Instead, embrace the constructive element. Anger involves fear – fear our needs aren't being met, fear we're losing someone, fear we're being taken advantage of, and so on. Pinpoint the fear and face it, and you'll be better equipped to deal constructively with both the fear and the anger.

FEAR

Instead of letting fear inhibit your creativity, think through it constructively. In so doing, you turn its energy around, enabling you to use it positively. This summons up courage that you may never have suspected you possessed. You do possess it. Use it to rout fear and release your creativity to sing and fly and dance whichever way is right for you.

GUILT

- ▸ Perhaps you feel guilty you're not as creative or accomplished as you've claimed.
- ▸ Perhaps you feel guilty you're stealing time for your creativity instead of giving it to your loved ones.

▶ Perhaps you feel guilty because you're so creative and your friends aren't.

▶ Perhaps you have done something mean or otherwise awful.

There are many ways people feel guilty and all can stunt their creativity. Guilt eats you up and depresses your zest for life. If you have done something terrible, make amendments or atone for it by doing something constructively good. Let yourself off the hopeless, useless hook of guilt by remembering...

▶ you are creative – if you're not as accomplished as you've claimed, you can be if you put the effort in

▶ you will give better-quality time to your nearest and dearest if you are personally fulfilled by your creativity.

▶ not shining creatively because your friends don't will not help them; shining creatively is your rightful destiny and may just help them, too

▶ we can't live a blameless life – but we can try to live as compassionately and as well as possible, both now and in the future.

RESENTMENT

We can spend our lives feeling resentful for this and that – and to what purpose? It does no good whatsoever. Do yourself, everyone around you and your creativity a huge favour: have a cool, calm think to see if the alleged cause gives genuine cause for offence. If so, deal with it sensibly and constructively if you can. If that's not possible in the circumstances, or if you realize you've got things out of perspective and proportion, decide firmly that you're going to let the resentment go. Either way you'll blow it out of your life and your creative aura.

TURNING NEGATIVE EMOTIONS AROUND

In acknowledging negative emotions, facing them and as best as possible dealing constructively with their cause, you are dealing creatively with them. In the process you get to know yourself better. That deepens and extends your creativity. It's a wonderful kind of alchemy. Out of the discomfort and trauma you mine creative gold.

You can use negative emotion to inspire, flood and energize your creative output, just as you can the positive ones such as exuberance, joy and love. Whether it involves passive or active anger, you can use it to fire up your creativity. In letting it flow out safely through your creative work or play, you defuse it, allowing you to think through the causes of your annoyance or outrage constructively and to seek solutions and better ways forward. In the process, your creativity will tell you a lot about yourself, your passion and the situation as a whole.

How being creative can heal or even pre-empt depression

When you set your emotions free to work in tandem with your creativity, it absorbs them and uses them for inspiration and energy. As you work, experience the feeling of being swept along in the flow. It might be anything from a sense of deep peace to a furious, driven demand. Your experience will depend on your mood and any emotions that are surfacing. At the time and/or afterwards, you may have a sense of understanding, relief or perhaps euphoria. In a way, what you produce is immaterial. The momentum and deeply personal heart of the journey are in themselves cathartic and often transformational.

However you use your creativity, the normal advice is to keep all your work. If, like me, you're so prolific you'd need a mansion to house your output in, this won't be realistic. Instead, I suggest you keep the work that

▶ you like aesthetically
▶ continues to move you
▶ reminds you of the emotional journey you took in the making of it
▶ you find particularly interesting in other ways.

That way, you can refer to it whenever you need solace, a sense of emotional enrichment or the inspirational reminder of seeing the impact of creative flow. You can also, of course, if your work is perishable, preserve it by taking photos or writing about it.

It's important not to be so technically critical of your finished work that you spoil the experience you've had. Yes, there's a place for criticism, of course: sometimes you will want and need to review it with a constructively critical eye to keep up the momentum of improvement and development. But allow yourself to fall in love with your work unreservedly and it will add a wonderful dimension to your life.

Practise the following exercise often:

Try this
1 Choose something you've produced that you like (it could be an actual artwork, a photo of visual work, some writing, music, etc.).
2 Pay attention to it with the relevant senses.
3 Take time to take it in – just as you would in a gallery or at a concert etc.
4 Be aware of your feelings about it.
5 Be aware of the way you are resonating with it.
6 Let your heart go out to it with a wave of love – it is, after all, in a sense a part of you. (Many creative people feel their work is like a baby, it's so dear to them.)
7 Be glad for it. Feel the quiet happiness purring inside you, or the thrill of joy uplifting your spirits.
8 Give thanks for your creativity and know that it is always there for you.

Insight
When you honour your creativity in this way, you honour yourself. This is not only good for your self-esteem, it's vital. An appreciation of your innate creativity in tandem with a feel-good level of self-esteem is an elixir for personal fulfilment and contentment. It doesn't mean we become complacent – far from it. As we appreciate our creativity and feel good about ourselves, we naturally grow towards the sun. We look to use our creativity more, to do it justice by learning and developing, to live well and help others use their creativity… it's an ever-evolving process.

We don't need to be or even aspire to be like Leonardo da Vinci, J. K. Rowling, Donatella Versace or anyone else at the top of their creative pinnacle. For creativity shines through the simplest of ordinary lives on a day-to-day level that some might consider mundane. Never ever consider your creativity and your life to be mundane. You have a unique life and all you need to do to honour it is to show up each day willing and happy to think and live creatively and usefully in the way you can. One of my favourite quotes which I repeat over and over because it's so inspiring is this:

> **Asked why he worked so hard to move millions to action to help 'feed the world', Bob Geldof answered: 'Because I can.'**

When we do what we can, and are glad for it, depression flees.

Bringing in positive emotions to light up your creativity

Bringing in positive emotions is also a great way to crowd out negativity. And when you feel good in all kinds of positive moods and ways, there is another kind of alchemy at work:

▶ Feel and revel in appreciation for the gifts of life, including creativity.
▶ Feel gladness and awe for your luck in being alive (the odds against the fertilized egg that became you surviving were billions to one against – how awesome is that?).
▶ Give yourself a moment now and then to let your happiness soar into joy.
▶ Feel the joy coursing through you now.
▶ Know that the flow of energy you're experiencing will manifest itself in your creativity.
▶ At any time of day whether you're working or relaxing, and whether your creativity is active or lying fallow, you can also think of and summon any of the following emotions/feelings to oust negativity:
  ▷ **hope** – whatever befalls us, hope holds our hand
  ▷ **optimism** – look on the bright side and for the best in everyone and every situation.
  ▷ **inspiration** – look, look, look for inspiration; it's in this book, it's in your life, it's in the world around you – all you have to do is notice it and get aboard
  ▷ **confidence** – know that you are strong and competent – you are!
▶ Trust in the energy of the world and the goodness and creativity that flows through it to energize you and look after you.
▶ Be glad, again and always, for the gift of life and creativity.
▶ Delight in life and see the magic.

Embracing practicalities to free you to be creative

HEALTH

The subject of health is rarely considered in relation to creativity. It needs to be because feeling below par physically or emotionally clips your creative wings and can keep you grounded. Look after your **body's health** – and to a surprising degree your **mental health**, too – by eating well, exercising regularly and making sure you have plenty of rest and relaxation.

Take an interest in the way the **food groups** affect your energy levels, creative flow and mood. I rarely feel like doing anything creative when I've had a big meal and I'm most likely to be inspired and get into flow easily and happily when I have an empty stomach or have eaten lightly. I prefer to eat a light, meatless lunch and to have my main meal later in the evening when I know I shall be relaxing afterwards. Other people find that by 'grazing' throughout the day they keep their blood sugar level consistent along with their inspiration and productivity. Eat the way that feels right for you and your creative flow.

Regular exercise has a big impact on the stream of energy, too. If ever I begin to flag, it's often because I've been still for too long. Even getting up and walking around the room for a few minutes will help. Better still take a break and go outside for a brisk ten-minute walk.

If your energy level is very impaired, you may feel so down and tired all you want to do is lie on a sofa or bed. If this happens, unless you have reason to need a good rest (in which case a catnap is an excellent idea), galvanize yourself into action:

▶ If you are hungry, eat a protein snack or a couple of pieces of fruit. Then imagine the energy it gives coursing through you! (It helps if you are old enough to remember Popeye with his beloved spinach that gave him immediate strength.)

▶ Do something uplifting. For instance, you could phone someone who always gives your spirits a lift, look at something that will inspire you like a favourite painter's work, or do something kind for someone.

▶ Do something physically active. You could wash the kitchen floor, for instance, do some gardening or clear some clutter.

All of these have an extraordinarily fast effect in raising your spirits, giving you a new flush of energy and new creative zest, too.

Insight

Looking after our health makes creative sense. To a large extent, we are what we eat. Food is our fuel so we need to make sure it's top quality and the right kind for our individual system and metabolism. That enables all our cells including the brain's to thrive and replenish. Exercise keeps our muscles supple and fit and our circulation in good order and that has a direct impact, too, on creativity since it delivers oxygen and feel-good hormones to the brain.

TECHNICAL SKILLS

The knowledge or fear that our technical skills aren't up to scratch to service our creativity can have a detrimental effect on it in various ways:

▶ A feeling of incompetence can deter you from starting being creative.

▶ A lack of the skill necessary to execute a creative project successfully could impede or stop progress.

▶ A lack of sufficient expertise makes it all too easy to give up altogether, telling yourself you're not 'good enough' to do it.

▶ You might even cite insufficient skill or experience as a form of self-defence to save you from effort.

There is a solution but perhaps because it's so glaringly obvious we take fright and run from it. Please don't! Face it and run *with* it and it will have a miraculous effect on your creativity, confidence and perhaps your whole life. It is simply this:

Learn, practise, get experience, develop...

You don't have to make a monumental effort all at once and instantly learn skills and gain experience. Taking it step by step will get you there in all good time and be enjoyable, too. You can also learn in whatever ways best suit you. Although the style of teaching at school didn't suit me very well, I've thoroughly enjoyed studying at college and university as a mature student. Try it – you may, like me, find that it seems so much easier than it did years ago. Perhaps you can source and choose all kinds of practical workshops and courses. Or another possible learning curve is with someone who is prepared to pass on their knowledge and skills on a one-to-one basis.

However you approach it, learning will feed your creativity in your life generally as well as enabling you to master a particular subject. When you learn with others, you have the bonus of meeting like-minded people and probably being inspired by them, too. Practice takes the knowledge and skills forward, experience comes in time, and your creativity and expertise will constantly be developing. Justifiably, you will feel proud of yourself as your knowledge widens and deepens. All in all, it will be very satisfying.

And all this because of a simple decision to learn and to improve your skills. You're never too old – we can be creative right through our lives and continually learning and developing. It feels good and it sweeps away all those 'I'm not much good at it' blocks and defences. You are creative. You have ability. Develop it. It will be fun!

FINANCES

Money, or rather the lack of it, is another block against creativity that we erect for ourselves. As we saw in Chapter 1, we can convince ourselves there's something external we need before we can let our creativity flow – be it a room, time or money – and money gets blamed for the first two barriers, too.

One solution might be to save up for a studio or office, or so that you can take a year's sabbatical to follow your creative dream. That's OK, but please don't let it mean you'll tread water creatively while you're waiting to save the desired amount. With a little thought and ingenuity (which you have plenty of because you're a creative person), you can devise ways to be creative in your present circumstances or by slightly modifying them to suit. Be creative whatever is or isn't happening in your life. Just get on with it. You will blossom.

Another money block that holds people back is the fear: 'I can't afford XYZ.' Fair enough – only a lucky few have the spare cash to rush out and equip themselves there and then for their creative plans and projects in one fair swoop. But there is a solution. *Beg!* Creative people love to help kindred spirits. I've been given so many brushes by other artists – cast-offs often but I'm not proud – that I've rarely had to buy any. On the paint front, I started with some old paints once used by my dad. Over the years, gifts and whatever purchases I've been able to afford gradually added to my present rainbow of colours. People will look at my stash in amazement and say: 'Gosh, you've got heaps of paint!' It certainly has accumulated, not because I have inexhaustible funds but because of the generosity of others and a certain amount of saving and budgeting, too.

Like anything else, we can budget, plan, save and prioritize to get the tools we need for our creativity. It takes determination and decision. Life will do the rest – just as people give me brushes and paint as gifts on special occasions, so people will get to know what you'd like for your birthday or whenever.

A last thought on the budgeting front. It's surprising what you can save with just a little sensible and easy thrift. I've cut back on all kinds of things I used to thoughtlessly spend money on. For instance:

▶ If you're going out, take lunch with you rather than buy it.
▶ Always take a flask of coffee, too. As an artist friend said: 'Two or three pounds for a cuppa? You're joking – that will buy some paint!'
▶ Read newspapers on line and listen to the wonderful Radio 4 to keep up to speed with news and interesting features.
▶ Books aren't an extravagance as they'll feed your zest for life along with your creativity. Help pay for them by putting them straight back for sale on the Internet as soon as you've read them.
▶ Ask everyone you know for their money-saving tips.

By being careful and prioritizing what you spend, you can afford what your creativity needs.

Sideways thinking about your talents and ambitions

Sheer logistics can be an effective deterrent to your pursuing a particular creative path. You may feel, for example, that, because there's bound to be so many people with the same idea as you, there's little point in even trying.

It's sensible to be pragmatic. For everyone who reaches the peak in any field, there are many – perhaps thousands – whose talent equals or even surpasses theirs. When a creative destination is so heavily oversubscribed, many people, however able, however determined, won't make it.

You may want to try in any case and you may certainly have the luck and opportunity that complements your ability and resolve and carries you through. But, if not, or if you simply don't want to set yourself up for likely disappointment in the first place, it doesn't mean you have to give up on your creative flair and dream. Creativity, loved and encouraged, is strong, vibrant and, of its very nature, creative! So when thwarted or wary of pursuing one route, you can explore other options, thinking sideways and every which way to satisfy your longing and your gut feeling that this is the area you are meant to be in.

Doing different things to free and fire your creativity

Another way to dislodge any creative block is to stop trying to make yourself get through it and instead walk away from the project altogether. Don't worry – it needn't be permanent and it could greatly strengthen and reinforce your long-term commitment to your goal. When we give something its freedom, if it's right for it to come back to us, it will do so of its own volition. The renewed connection, being mutual, will be all the deeper and better for the time apart.

Meanwhile, satisfy your need to be creative in another way or several. Go off at a tangent or jump into something completely different. Exploring your potential to learn about, practise and enjoy other things inspires you on many fronts. It may lead full circle back to your original creative path, or it may introduce you to another you love as much or even more. Along the way, you'll find the new path or pastime enriching and fulfilling in its own right.

It's similar to the way a holiday recharges your batteries and renews enthusiasm jaded by day-after-day contact. Taking a break is interesting and therapeutic and you may well find, when you come back to it, that the block has disappeared and your creativity is free-flowing.

Letting go of envy and jealousy

I suspect we've all been there: someone we know is being amazingly creative and perhaps reaping financial success or professional acclaim and we so wish it could be happening to us! Envy and jealousy are all natural reactions, but we don't have to succumb. Far better not to, because not only do we feel beastly but they can scupper our creativity, too.

So deal with any of these negative, potentially block-forming feelings before they gain sway. Here's how:

> Try this
> 1 Notice your feeling and admit to it.
> 2 Remind yourself that it's a natural and normal reaction but you can control and defuse it.
> 3 Decide to be glad for the person.
> 4 Warmly congratulate them and wish them well both in practice and in your mind.
> 5 Recognize how thinking 'good for them' feels good to you.
> 6 Remember that your creativity is wonderful, too, and unique to you. It is yours.
> 7 Own it, value it and be glad for it.
> 8 Determine not to waste any more psychic, creative and emotional energy on the negative feelings.
> 9 Channel it positively into the joy of your creativity.
> 10 Feel it flowing through you.

We need to run through this cleansing exercise whenever envy crops up because it's at best a nuisance for our overall contentment and at worse detrimental to our creativity. Freeing ourselves of envy is wonderfully purifying and means you can get on with your life and your joyful participation in your own creativity.

> **Insight**
> The more you get used to dismantling your blocks, the easier and quicker it becomes – so much so that very soon it is practically an instant reaction. As time goes by, you'll take this a stage further, realizing that not only do we not have to let blocks hinder us, but we can stop them arriving in the first place. It's just a matter of being alert to them and saying 'no' to the block and 'yes' to your creativity.

6 POINTS OF REFLECTION

1 Keep working on your self-esteem. Your creativity needs you to value yourself and, in doing so, you will build up confidence in yourself and your abilities.

2 Be aware of your emotions and realize that you can often manage and defuse negative ones by using their energy in your creativity.

3 Let your creativity heal you when you're down or depressed. It has huge healing power.

4 Use positive emotions to light up your life – and your creativity. Feel them, appreciate them, share them with others.

5 Be practical. What are the needs of your creativity and how can you supply them?

6 Try different ways to let the flow of your creativity run smoothly. Remember you have your own unique creativity and be glad for it. Catch and throw out negative thoughts about others' abilities – they have their story, you have yours – and yours is, in its own way, great.

6

....

Finding your muse

In this chapter you will learn:
- *how time and place can be your muse*
- *to use all kinds of media to uplift you and give you ideas*
- *to relish the creative richness of silence and solitude*
- *to discover the joy of a beloved human being or pet as your muse.*

Anything and anyone you love and which or who inspires you can be
your muse. It isn't just that you like, love or dote on it or them, which
of course is a great emotional experience in its own right. It's that,
in lighting up your life, it not only releases your creativity but gives
it wings to fly. Throughout the book and throughout your life you'll
recognize all kinds of things or muses that strike a chord with you,
but in this chapter we'll look at some of the best-known ones.

_____

Discovering the magic of time

One of the wonderful things about creativity is its ability to adapt to
whatever time is available. Creativity is flexible, abundant, generous.
It's with you every step of the way through life – all you need to do
is notice it or ask it to appear and there it is. Embrace it and it's the
most wonderful muse.

I've only recently realized that time needn't limit us. We can use it
instead as our muse – an inspiration to fire us up and get us going.
But how can that be if you're so busy you haven't time to think, or
have an idea, let alone do something creative?

But the 'time muse' doesn't need hours, or even many minutes. It's
there in the *moments* – and we all have those, however busy we are.
And it's in those moments that some of the best ideas come. It doesn't

even need to be a moment of peace. An idea may flash into your consciousness when you're talking with someone, getting on a bus – doing anything, anywhere. Certainly, you might not have time to do anything other than make a note of it on paper or in your memory, but that's OK – you can attend to it later when you do have time to consciously process it. Meanwhile your subconscious will be already doing that.

I'm repeatedly surprised by this phenomenon when I come to do something that started as an idea months or even years ago. I'll feel daunted as I think: 'Oh no – there's so much background work to do before I can make a start.' But then the information, thoughts, tools and techniques will all start to assemble as if of their own accord. Yes, of course, there is still groundwork to be done – but it's more a case of filling in the gaps and assembling the pieces of the patchwork into a complete picture than starting completely from scratch.

You will find the same thing. Your mind will take that first moment for the idea. Then it will process the idea, often unbeknown to you, watching out for things that appertain to it.

The same happens as you consciously pay attention to the idea and, whenever you've the time, start work for real. Your mind draws more and more apt stuff towards you. It's quite extraordinary. You'll open a newspaper or magazine to an article that's so spot-on informative you can't believe it. Or you might see the name and phone number of a company that will be hugely helpful to you on the back of the car you're following. It can happen in all kinds of ways and, though you could put it down to coincidence or serendipity, I don't think it is. I think our consciousness – or subconscious – has amazing power to bring us what we need, when we need it, and using as much or as little time as we have.

We'll take a look again at this alchemy later in the book. When it happens to you, notice and appreciate its appearance, and delight in it – it is a very real treasure.

And do remember, too, that, despite a busy life, we can often make time for hobbies with a bit of thought and determination. You could, for instance, start writing the book you've in mind now rather than waiting until you retire. So, instead of assuming you need a long swathe of free time for it, engineer a regular space each day – even an hour will do. You can set the alarm clock earlier to give yourself an early-morning creative slot, or cut out a non-essential pastime. Use the time to plan your book and then write it. A novel may seem an impossible prospect if you look at it as, say, 80,000 words. But if you write 250 words a day in your four-days-a-week slot, that's 1,000 words a week. In less than a year and a half your book will be finished!

So, in a nutshell...

▶ elbow a small chunk of time for yourself in your schedule
▶ step by regular step use it to progress your idea
▶ in between, use any moments you may have, however brief, to welcome thoughts and ideas – your subconscious will continue to process them even when you're busy with other things.

This way your creative project will get done and be an enjoyable and immensely satisfying part of your life. The time is there. Harness it!

Insight
Most creative activity is doable, however busy you are. The most important thing is to show up for your creativity regularly, take it little by little and, above all, nurture it with your care and enthusiasm.

Discovering the right place

Is there a 'right' place to let your creativity flow? We probably all dream of the ideal location to follow our creative dream. It could be a home that would nurture your imagination and even be your muse – perhaps a cottage in beautiful countryside with amazing views or an apartment in a buzzy city that's full of other creative people, like New York perhaps. Or you might harbour a vision of a dedicated study or studio, perfect for ensconcing yourself in as your projects come to fruition.

What would be the ideal place for your creativity?

It helps to have a clear picture because this makes it easier to decide whether or not you really need it. A vague longing doesn't help you to be creative and may be yet another block to it. Knowing exactly what you would like gives you two possibilities, one or both of which will inspire and further your creativity.

First, it may be that once you know what you would ideally like, you'll see that, actually, it isn't essential and might not even be conducive to creative flow. For several years I'd thought how lovely it would be to have a studio where I could paint to my heart's content and leave all my gear out instead of having to constantly tidy up. In my last home, I finally made the dream a reality, converting an old stone shed into a spacious studio. In went my easel and all my stuff.

The strange thing was that I painted there only once but gravitated almost instantly back to the familiarity of the kitchen–living room, with its big table and the view from the windows. The studio was extremely useful for other things but creatively inspiring, much to my surprise, it wasn't. It turned out that my *familiar* painting place was my muse. Even in my new home, I still paint at that table, now at one end of the sitting room. It's comfortable and I like it, even though I still have to tidy up at the end of a session. No longer do I lust after a dedicated studio because I know all too well I don't need it.

However, many people love having a 'room of their own', dedicated to their creative flow. For them it is worth, if not essential, doing everything they can to make it possible because it is effectively their muse.

Second, the area where you live and/or work may impact on your creativity, too. Even when I was a little girl, living on the outskirts of a town, I dreamed of living either by the sea or in the country. As an adult, I realized it was so important to me I worked towards it. I can't tell you the number of times I was told by estate agents that the kind of situation I wanted wasn't possible but I somehow nonetheless always managed to find somewhere lovely. But many creative people I know don't mind where they live, so it's a very individual decision.

Have a think about it to see what's right for you:

> **Try this**
> 1 Sit and be at peace.
> 2 Visualize your ideal creative area, geographically.
> 3 Would you really be more creative if you lived there?
> 4 Now see your ideal room.
> 5 Would you really use it and would it increase your creative flow?

If the answer to one or both is 'yes', use your creativity, logic and determination to move you in the right direction to realize your dream. Please don't let finance be a daunting obstacle. I know two people who each longed to live somewhere beautiful – in the centre of London and by a river respectively – but thought they couldn't possibly afford such sought-after locations. One now lives in a houseboat with a permanent mooring on the Thames, the other in a narrow boat on a beautiful navigable canal in the heart of the country. Another friend who thought she could never afford the office space she wanted in her city was offered the use of someone's annexe in return for a few hours' help. Solutions come if we know what we want and pay attention to the opportunities that arise.

However, be aware that an apparent longing for 'the right place' could mask the fear of being creative in practice.

CASE STUDY

Karen told me she would never be able to write while she had so many work and family demands. She said she needed time to herself in the country. Then her husband surprised her on her birthday with a gift of a long stay in a beautiful rural cottage so that she could write to her heart's content. The gift did indeed prove valuable, but in a very different way. Karen realized, once ensconced in her country idyll, that this longed-for chance to get going was all too much. To her dismay she hardly wrote anything. Returning, she realized that the way forward was at home with her family, setting aside an hour a day to work on her idea. She now works steadily and not only enjoys it but is thrilled with her progress after so many years of procrastination.

Even if we don't actually need to live in a particular place, though, certain spots do undoubtedly resonate with us creatively. Sometimes a place will become a creative oasis simply because we've fostered a habit of writing or thinking there. Famously, for example, J. K. Rowling wrote much of her first Harry Potter book in a café. Instead of encroaching on her creativity, the hustle, bustle and atmosphere of the café cradled and enabled it.

Usually, though, it tends to be a beauty spot – somewhere, for example, with a lovely view. Throughout my life, wherever I've lived, I've loved several such special places where I like to sit and look, soaking in the beauty. When you find somewhere that seems to speak to your soul it gives you solace, a sense of perspective, creative sustenance and, often, inspiration, too. Churches and churchyards also often have this sense of wondrous peace that puts us in touch with our creative energy. Gardens, with their beauty, interest, peace and growth, are amazingly good places to tune into it, too, as are seashores and riverbanks. We'll look again at this link between places, spirituality and creativity in Chapter 9.

As ever, finding and recognizing a place that can be your muse is about understanding yourself, facing reality and at the same time honouring your dreams. In this climate of love and care, your creativity will flourish and so will you.

Giving yourself the right tools

In Chapter 6 we looked at ways to provide ourselves with the equipment we need for our creativity. There are three valuable benefits:

1 It feels great and is practical to have at our fingertips the gear that will help us work as well and pleasurably as possible.
2 It's also a way of honouring ourselves and our work. Just as a craftsman values his tools, so should all other creative people. It's good for your self-esteem as your creativity is an innate part of your being.
3 Well-chosen equipment that feels good to use can in itself be a muse, inspiring you to work, to have new ideas and to accept their challenge to gain experience and increase your skill.

Discovering the magic of inspirational outings

It's easy to become so engrossed in your creative pursuits that you rarely go out and do something different. If you recognize in yourself this tendency to become absorbed in your creativity, determine right now to regularly invite yourself out of your rut, however fulfilling it seems, and take a look at another vista. Think of it as a gift to yourself that will pay dividends in your creative flow.

It's easy to become so absorbed in our creative work and interests that we rarely do anything else, but be careful not to let this happen as new experiences and vistas always in some way give us inspiration, new perspectives and lift our spirits, too.

Ensure you give yourself the precious gift of at least one of the following at least once a week:

▶ Meet up with lively-minded people. Whether or not they see themselves as creative, the interplay of your thoughts, ideas and impressions will resonate with your brightness and encourage it to shine.

▶ Go to an art exhibition or a museum of interest to you. Looking at beautiful or interesting work and objects is manna to the creative soul.

▶ Go dancing. Movement, rhythm and music lift the spirit in a very special way and make our creativity dance.

▶ Sing with others. Belting out hymns in church, singing with a choir or a band, or having a ball singing at a karaoke session all have an amazingly feel-good effect – better, and far better *for* you, than any recreational drug, and incredibly inspirational on the creative front.

▶ You're already exercising regularly (see Chapter 5). Now and then vary the surroundings. Walk, swim, play sport, whatever it is you do, go somewhere different to do it. New surroundings interest the mind... and needless to say your creativity, too.

▶ Have a new and/or exciting experience. Make a list of all the things you've always wanted to do (or do again) and have a go. It could be travelling somewhere you've never been before, skydiving, going to the opera... all manner of things. The excitement, interest and the wow factor will give your creativity a tremendous boost.

▶ Do something you love but rarely treat yourself to. The only criterion is that it's something self-indulgent and, to you, totally gorgeous. I did a straw poll with some friends and they came up: spending a morning at a favourite shopping centre; having a massage; going horse riding; spending a whole afternoon reading.

Insight

While your creative treat might have an obvious connection to your creativity, like a painter visiting an art exhibition, it may be something completely unrelated. The magic of a personal treat like this is the way that, besides being pleasurable, it sets your creative antennae vibrating. You'll feel vibrant and inspired to progress existing ideas and you may find new ones popping into your mind, too. It's a holiday – a great way to recharge your creative energy and give it fresh scope to play with, too.

Using all kinds of media to uplift you and give you ideas

Books, poetry, films, television programmes, newspapers, the Internet, music, art – all the different forms of these media are full of information that may be useful to your creativity. In another way, they can also be a muse – a source of inspiration with perhaps the power to guide you, too.

Think, for example, of the books that have moved you not only emotionally but somehow raised within you a surge of longing to be creative in some way, or perhaps even directly stimulated fresh ideas.

It happens to me all the time. The very first books that inspired me creatively were C. S. Lewis's *Chronicles of Narnia* and throughout my life they've continued to inspire me whenever I think of them. For instance, if I go for a walk through a wood, brushing through the branches, I'll 'become' Lucy in *The Lion, the Witch and the Wardrobe* when she enters the world of Narnia through an enchanted forest. In a moment the beauty and wonder of the books come back to me and, with them, a realization of the astonishing power of our creativity to imagine other dimensions.

Today in my reading it continues to surprise me how many books have a similar 'charisma' and give me the sense that the author or characters are taking me by the hand to lead my creativity forwards.

And then there's the creative joy of films. Isn't it good when a character or the story deeply moves and inspires you? Again it's the feeling of engagement. We learn something and perhaps gain a deeper understanding of the human mind and the way we relate to others and the world around us. At the same time, the imagination or other creative talent behind it speaks to us through the medium of the film. A sign that something shines in this way for you is when you not only feel enthralled at the time, but long afterwards find yourself recalling scenes and dialogue.

Do music or paintings 'do it' for you? Perhaps, like me, you love the way certain music affects you emotionally and fills you with a longing to reach up and out to others, often inspiring me to be creative in some way. And paintings – it may rarely happen that one resonates with you but when it does it's like being flooded with a revitalizing wave of creative flow. It lifts your spirits and makes you long to interpret the colours and forms in your own work.

Which creative media affect you? The more you think about this, the more different media will come to mind and the more you'll notice them from now on.

One of the great things about the whole gamut of creative media is that through your own creativity you can connect with others across social divides, decades and even centuries. It's as though you feel the emotions that played through the mind of the author or film-maker, poet or lyricist, artist or composer, producing a powerful muse that speaks to you now.

The same sense of creative connection can come to you and inspire you through so many things:

Try this
1 Note down the books or other media that have strongly affected you and given you a creative energy charge.
2 Recall the feeling that each awoke in you.
3 Reflect that you are a highly creative being.
4 Be alert for the charge of energy that runs through you.
5 Consider how the link you sense with the author or maker is inspiring you.
6 Sense or imagine how the author or the story is beckoning you to release your creativity.
7 Engage with their energy and see yourself and your creative flow as part of the stream of creative consciousness that is a part of you and our world.

It's really good to refresh your memories of the artworks, films and books that have inspired you, and to look out for new ones in the making. In Chapter 2 we looked at how useful scrapbooks, notebooks and day boards are as an instant source of inspiration. Whenever you remember or come across something new that has a cathartic creative effect, make a note and keep it handy for easy access. At any time you can then revisit it and relive the inspiration, enabling the resurgence of a feeling of creative start-up or flow.

Insight

Storytelling and information giving – when they are done well – not only interest and inform us, but open up or deepen another element of our lives. Never stop reading, learning, watching dramas and documentaries and appreciating anything made with creative love and endeavour. Think how you relate to these and wonder at the joy of connection with your own creativity that they enable. They are a powerful muse!

Relishing the creative richness of silence and solitude

Perhaps the most necessary muse for most of us is quiet time for reflection. In today's high-tech world we stream in so much information from so many sources that we can suffer from an information overload that is anathema to creativity. Sometimes, certainly, a buzzy flow of information can be creatively exciting, but be careful not to overdo it as a constant flow has the opposite effect of dulling original imagination and inspiration. Research has shown that our brains change when taking in too much information on an ongoing basis, balancing this over-activity by repressing the area that controls creativity.

So with computers and electronic forms of communication, bear in mind that moderation is essential for your creativity to spark easily and flow well.

Unless others understand your vital need for silence, you'll need solitude, too. Uninterrupted peace and quiet give us the opportunity to let our thoughts range where they will, and to allow ideas and inspirations to come through clearly. Just a little time may be all it takes to enter the quiet place inside your mind where you make yourself available to connect with your creativity and let it flow.

Four excellent conduits provide just the right conditions for the wonderful muse of peace:

1 **Exercise** that doesn't require thought is a great opportunity to tune in. Walking and swimming, for example, give peace for contemplation, but it can be any gentle activity that doesn't demand conversation and mental concentration.

2 **Meditation** is another way and is extremely relaxing, too.

3 Once you're in your seat and the car, bus, train or plane is on the move, **travel** is an interlude that's especially conducive to contemplation. Resist that temptation to listen to the radio or attention-seeking music. Enjoy the creative ride!

4 Sit still at home, **doing nothing at all**. This may seem very strange at first, as most of us have got into the habit of always doing something even when we're relaxing. Breathe slowly, let go of any tension in your muscles or mind and simply be still.

Any muse, but perhaps the one of peace in particular, enables us to connect with something beyond our physical being. It feels as though you've reached a different element or dimension of life. Your creativity links with this spirituality and takes off – soaring as though meant to be. It *is* meant to be because it's a part of you – a gift of life and joy.

In Chapter 9 we'll look more extensively at solitude, silence and spirituality and explore the knack of meditation. For the moment, simply enjoy the experience. You may like to note your impressions in your free-flow writing practice.

Letting a beloved human being or pet be your muse

Over the centuries many creative people have chosen or found a person or pet to be their muse. Much of Elgar's music was inspired by the women he fell in love with, for instance, and Picasso's imagination and talent were also stimulated by his girlfriends and wives.

The feeling of being in love is undoubtedly often creatively powerful. Fortunately, although the in-love stage of a relationship tends to be temporary, we have the ability to recall the feeling, so it can spark our creativity over and over again. Ongoing love, too, is a powerful creative drive for many of us. We may enjoy pleasing our partners and other loved ones with our work, be encouraged by them or perhaps pace our creativity with theirs.

I well remember how, when in a relationship with a man who was as or more creative than I, I found his creativity and talent and my striving to match it incredibly inspiring and, in a sense, intoxicating. Just like our rapport, the creativity it inspired in me was fun, exciting and satisfying. Life is calmer now, but he is still a muse I can draw on – because just thinking of that time and the buzz we shared can be a catalyst for me to get to work on an inspirational idea.

Today my sister and certain of my friends, all highly creative, are each my muse and I treasure them. You'll probably know or find this spark, too, within your close circle of loved ones. You can recognize them by the way you feel uplifted and encouraged to let your creativity flow when you're with them or communicating through emails or phone calls. Enjoy them and cherish them for they give you such a wonderful gift.

Bless the person who is your muse, the passion and/or love you share and your alchemical creative interaction with them. It's very special.

Over and over again, I also see how animals – our much loved pets – can be a tremendous muse. As I watch, for instance, my young dog growing up, her personality and love of life makes me dance for joy, and this feeds directly into my creativity. My cat is a dear creature, too. Her closeness and warmth and her astonishing beauty inspire me to paint her – so far I've been very inept at this but hopefully I will one day do her justice. Horses are an ongoing muse for me, providing a rich vein of inspiration. Their characters – each one unique – and the sense of their spirituality somehow touch mine and it's astonishingly cathartic in releasing my creativity. I very much enjoy bringing something of their magic to my work.

Insight

Be aware of whom and what inspires you in a particular, joyous way. Appreciate them and take the gift of inspiration and encouragement they give you and use it to the full. Feel the interplay of creative energy that flows between you. Feel, too, the heritage of creative people and their muse down through the centuries and know that you, now, are part of it. Feel how good it is. Be grateful for the gift. Be glad. Enjoy!

6 POINTS OF REFLECTION

1 Time is astonishingly flexible. Sometimes we need surprisingly little time for a creative thought or plan to come through, or even to complete a complex project. Let your creativity flow and time will open up for it.

2 Find places which appeal to your creativity. Be aware of any that inspire you or where you feel you can work comfortably. Creativity enjoys a sense of place.

3 You are a creative person and deserve the right, good-quality tools to let your creativity work well.

4 Have you had an outing recently for you and your creativity? Remember how inspiring it is to go out and about. Inspiration comes when we explore.

5 Keep in creative contact with other creative people around the globe through the wealth of media available to us. Take time, too, to be quiet and enjoy some time with yourself alone.

6 Be aware of people and animals who make your creativity dance with joy. Cherish them and keep company with them as often as you can.

7

··

Personal contacts

In this chapter you will learn how to unlock your creativity by:
- *listening to or talking with like-minded, creative people*
- *being part of a team*
- *forging and maintaining a one-to-one partnership*
- *being creative the way you want to be*
- *buffering and transforming others' negativity.*

Listening to or talking with like-minded, creative people

There's nothing like mixing with creative people for firing up your own creativity. It's a kind of alchemy again – as though your creative souls sparkle in the air separately at first as you recognize a common creative flair, and then are magnetized to each other and dance together for a while. Ideas flow and you both feel uplifted and energized, and when you part you look forward eagerly to riding on the wave of creativity you've mutually started.

Sometimes it happens out of the blue. I remember once, for instance, sharing a long car journey with Rita, who was then a new neighbour. My initial impression of her had been of an efficient, very focused businesswoman and I had no idea there was another, artistic and spiritual side to her. She, it turned out later, had harboured a similarly incomplete impression of me. But, released from the confines of social small talk, we quickly discovered a mutual love of art, craft, meditation and healing. So began an inspiring friendship of several years until sadly our lives took us in different directions. But, as we saw in the last chapter, memory can energize creativity in the present, and recalling her creative zest now reminds me of how our conversations and mutual encouragement so often inspired my writing and painting and her various creative projects.

You will already know who inspires you in your circle of friends, family and colleagues. Treasure them and make sure you reciprocate by uplifting them, too, and giving them confidence in their own creativity. And be aware that others whom you don't know as well on the creative front may also have a rich creative seam in their genetic make-up even if they're not fully aware of it themselves. See if you can be a catalyst for an epiphany for them personally and also for a creative rapport between you. It feels great to help others this way and, even if nothing sparks immediately, you may just plant a seed of inspiration in them that will one day germinate and grow to blossom and fruition.

Insight

Most of us, however independent and loving of solitude we might be, need contact with and the company of like-minded creative souls. There are so many great pluses: you can give each other solace when the creative path of either one of you hits a rough patch, comfort when one of you feels unsure, inspiration to try new things, and ongoing stimulus and encouragement. Then, of course, there's the pure pleasure of your rapport.

Try this

I'd like you to:

1 make a list of people with whom you have a creative rapport
2 add some people who may have a hidden but rich creative seam
3 contact them one by one and make a time to talk and, if possible, meet face to face
4 feel the buzz between you
5 let ideas flow
6 encourage and take a keen interest in their ideas and work at least as much as they do in yours
7 think warmly of them and of their hopes and achievements. Firmly banish any negative competitive thoughts, though it's fine to nurture a healthy competitive spirit if it will spur you both on.

Bear these people in mind later when you're next being creative and let the energy that buzzes between you when you're in contact continue to spark your flow in the moment.

Meeting with other creative people in a mutually encouraging atmosphere is a great tonic for your soul as well as your creativity. Recent research on wellbeing found that getting together regularly with people whose company you enjoy has as big an effect on raising your happiness as doubling your salary!

Conversation that keeps going in different directions is part of this feel-good equation. As it flows, you attune to each other's thoughts and emotions, increasing both the camaraderie and the healing feeling of understanding and being understood. When you can bounce ideas about creativity around, too, you'll find the whole happiness effect is even greater and, of course, inspirational.

Being part of a team

Working in a creative environment where everyone's ingenuity and imagination is appreciated helps you draw creativity forth. Set in context with sound knowledge, expertise and experience, a fresh approach gives every project an interesting edge and often adds special promise and excitement, too. It goes full circle because, when you're part of a happy, enthusiastic team, you look forward to work every day and that fosters more creativity.

Two team tactics may apply in the workplace where creative demands are high:

1 brainstorming ideas *and*
2 a dedicated focus.

It's fun to brainstorm ideas and any one of your team might come up with a thought or proposal that perhaps wouldn't have occurred to you on your own. The success of **brainstorming** – an idea-seeking meeting where everyone attending is free to say whatever comes into their head – is an amalgam of relaxation, competition and serendipity:

▶ **You relax** as you know that all sorts of wacky ideas may be thrown into the pot, so you feel free to say whatever comes into your head. It's a great way of avoiding the self-consciousness that in a more formal meeting might hinder you and even lock up potentially terrific ideas because of the fear of seeming foolish.

- There's nothing like **healthy competition** among peers to extend your creativity to its limits as you search for an idea that will trump everyone else's. The encouragement your colleagues give you, and perhaps even the pressure they exert on you to come up with good ideas and inspired thought, works wonders in helping you produce the goods.
- The sheer chance element of the hotchpotch of ideas chucked into the ring may **serendipitously** trigger more ideas too.

A dedicated focus can also, in a different way, enable you to come up with original ideas, which may be spot on and fully formed already or which offer a great beginning that can be worked up later.

There is a current theory that brainstorming is not as successful in the business world as a more focused, linear search. I've found, working on various ideas and projects throughout my life, that the two techniques work well both on their own and together, and which you choose depends on the team and the kind of thoughts and ideas you're seeking.

The important and exciting thing is that, when everyone directs their minds at the same thing, you get an extraordinarily wide range of intelligence, ability and talent that can often combine to create amazing ideas as well as a trajectory of purpose and process that's itself creative and constructive.

The feeling of being part of a group, whether you're with colleagues or with like-minded people at a workshop or lecture, gives you a sense of belonging that cradles awakening creativity and encourages it to develop. You'll also pick up on the energy of the leader or facilitator of the group – if he or she is a good one – and on the buzz in the room, too.

There is something beguilingly inspiring about being with others on the same creative wavelength. Afterwards you'll feel relaxed and satisfied, yet with your antenna alert to the creativity you've experienced and been close to, ready for you to tune into again at any time.

Forging and maintaining a one-to-one creative partnership

A one-to-one creative union is another personal connection that offers rich rewards in its own way. It may exist in its own exclusive right when two otherwise unconnected people come together to discuss ideas, help make plans, develop a project, and/or edit or otherwise help improve each other's work. This often happens with script- or screenwriters. As you bounce ideas and, in this case, lines of dialogue between you, a flow of creativity develops that can speed work up and keep it fresh and lively, too.

The creative partnership can also be part of and greatly complement an existing friendship, business, or personal relationship or marriage. Here are three examples:

CASE STUDY

1 I've twice had the good fortune to work creatively with a business partner and even years later, as I write about it, I'm tingling with the memory of the zest, warmth and inspiration that sparked and flowed between us whenever we worked together. Today I'm fortunate to have a creative friend who enjoys helping me with my work and having me to work with his.

2 My sister and brother-in-law, both writers, edit each other's books as well as being a great listening board when exploring new ideas and ventures, and a great development team as they progress them.

3 Jeffrey, a successful artist, has three working friends, all painters like him. He spends a week or two with each of them at various times of the year, often travelling abroad to work in new surroundings. He not only enjoys their company as they paint together, but also values having like-minded 'arty' conversation, exchanging ideas and inspirations, and criticizing each other's work – positively and constructively of course!.

I emphasize the need for mutual encouragement in such one-to-one rapports. It's about offering suggestions rather than being bossy, finding something good to praise as well as talking about the changes you think will be beneficial. It's vital that you can trust each other, not just to be truthful, but to be supportive and heartening, too.

But apart from being an excellent mutual advice and support system, the sheer brilliance of such a relationship is the energy and inspiration that flows through it.

So it's well worth looking out for opportunities in your life and circle of friends, family and other contacts to initiate a creative connection. Good ways to discover if you have this kind of creative empathy are...

▶ **going for a long walk together** – there is something about the exercise, changing location, and opportunity for both individual contemplation and conversation that quickly develops any creative rapport you may have

▶ **having a go at doing some work together** – you may find you'd both like to do this on a regular basis. Even if this doesn't transpire, it's fun to work with someone else even if it's a one-off or occasional session. It saves you having to summon the energy to be creative all on your own.

Exercising and playing games and sports with others

Again, playing games and sports will have an energizing and beneficial effect on your creativity whether you play as a pair or in a larger team. Camaraderie, devising tactics, playing together – all these make your mind work and improve your blood circulation, and a side effect is a boost to your creativity.

A highly creative IT designer, Lucy, told me that she noticed a marked difference when she joined an aerobic dance exercise class instead of working out on her own at home: 'While I felt physically good after a half-hour session at home,' she said, 'there was something about doing the same movements with the group that transformed the experience. I'd get home afterwards with my mind in creative gear, buzzing with ideas and itching to at least jot them down and maybe even get started on them.' She figured it was the added pleasure of having company and sharing laughter that made the difference and added: 'It takes the high you get with aerobic exercise to another level, which seems to have a direct effect on your creativity.'

A lot of games and sports require ingenuity and imagination to do really well at them. So you're giving the sections of your brain that control creativity a good workout at the same time as your body.

The more you play a game, the more you use your muscles, the easier it becomes to do so; the better you get at it and the more pleasurable it becomes. It's much the same when you exercise your creativity and so, when you're playing sport and games that use your mind, you get a treble whammy of physical, mental and creative fitness.

Making music and dancing

You only have to watch the faces of the members of a band, orchestra or choir to see their delight in making music together. The more they enjoy this rapport, the more they strive to create more magic – whether it's through technique, style or sheer passion. And so their creativity and ability develops, giving more and more pleasure. It's the same with dancers. Yes, they may love dancing solo but to dance with someone or with a group again adds the delicious feeling of rapport and interaction to the joy of the music, movement and rhythm.

So, if you enjoy playing an instrument, singing or dancing, join with others in making or dancing to music and notice how it draws out the feeling of being creative, or of being even more creative than usual. Feel the buzz of the energy between you and the fun of harmonizing all your senses. Notice, especially, how you feel afterwards and, to save the feeling for later inspiration, record it:

Try this
You might like to draw or paint an impression of you and the others as you played, sang or danced together, or of your feelings during and afterwards. It can be as figurative or abstract as you wish. Let your hands move as they will so that it feels as though the paint, pencil or ink is flowing of its own accord onto the paper.

OR

Try this
Write about your experience immediately or in your free-flow writing in the morning. Tune into the creative energy you sensed. Recall how good it felt to be in tune – literally and metaphorically! – with the others.

Recently I watched a documentary about the rock band Queen, and the creative energy they shared seemed to be fairly rocking out of the television set, making me feel fantastic, too. If I felt like that just listening to Brian May and Roger Taylor talking about their love of making music, just think how wonderful it must be for them to share the high of playing together. Another part of the programme explored the band's love of writing songs together. Interestingly, they found that, when they decided to credit the songs to the band as a whole rather than the individual who had the idea or put most into it, they enjoyed the experience even more.

Once again it shows that, while competition can be an incentive to be creative, working as a team with others you respect and whose work you love may be an even greater one, as well as more relaxing and pleasurable. And a bonus of taking ego out of the creative equation is that, freed from its grasp and self-consciousness, each one of the team will have more energy and be more creative still.

Insight

Making and dancing to music with others have a vibrant energy that resonates between you. It generates creativity in both the interpretation and the passion you share. This energy flows between you and often lasts long afterwards in a feeling of buzzing creativity that fosters and feeds our other creative work and interests. Harmony, rhythm, joy, excitement and a feeling of creative flow – you stand to enjoy all of these as you make music or dance with others.

Laughing and having fun with others

Laughter is joyously cathartic on the creative front. It's as though, as your body shakes with mirth, it shakes your creativity up, too, throwing it into the arena and bidding you take notice of it and interact.

Having a good laugh with friends gives you a wonderful feeling of rapport as well. The warmth and positivity have a great effect on our innate creativity, complementing and encouraging it. But it doesn't work the same way with negative humour that's nastily sarcastic or cruel – it's the positivity of genuine feel-good fun or wit that resonates with our creativity and makes it fizz.

Cherish those friends and colleagues you laugh with. Recreate the natural joy of giggling you loved as a child.

Can you really 'manufacture' laughter? Absolutely. You can even do it on your own; acting out laughing aloud, you pretty soon get overtaken by the laughter and find it's for real. Try it – it's true! But it's even easier and more fun with others. Try to pick up on their humour. Show your appreciation not just by laughing but by continuing the joke by making, for instance, another wry comment or perhaps saying something ridiculous. Don't be frightened or self-conscious to laugh at your own humour – remember how infectious laughter is and just let go of your inhibitions and chuckle.

An exchange of humour and laughter is much like a good conversation – you listen and show your appreciation of what they've said by laughing and then say something funny yourself or feed them a line so they can continue to be amusing. Let yourself go and giggle, and enjoy the feeling of a wave of laughter flooding through you.

It feels so brilliant and, like music and dance, strikes a chord with our creativity. When we hit the high that laughter gives us, or find the satisfaction and warmth given by gentle humour, feel-good chemicals flood through us and reverberate with our creative ability and longings. It's like an alchemical reaction. Take advantage of it. After sharing laughter, do something creative – it could be whatever is your particular thing or something new. It could be anything from this book and probably many other forms of creativity I've missed or haven't mentioned. Take your pick and enjoy tapping the rich seam of creative gold that flows from laughing and having fun with friends.

Insight

Laughter shared with others has an energy of its own that will resonate with your creativity. Encourage it as often as possible and enjoy it to the full. Then let the wonderful feeling spur you into doing something creative and enjoy that, too. So much in life depends on us seizing opportunities and this is especially true of both laughter and creativity and the way they work in tandem, encouraging each other – and encouraging you!

Being creative the way you want to be

Everyone is creative, but unless you believe in your ability, you may not show or use it much. Building faith in yourself will go hand in hand with unlocking your creativity, but you can speed the process and give it an instant boost by behaving as though you are already highly creative and confident about being, for instance, very artistic or an 'ideas person'.

There's a vintage Tony Hancock film called *The Rebel* that, even as it hilariously mocks artistic delusion and pretentiousness, holds a seam of truth about creative confidence. Scorned by his wife, the character Hancock plays moves to Paris where he dons a beret and makes out he's a great artist. Soon he finds that his work is appreciated by the arty young of Paris, if not by the experts. Suddenly he *is* a famous artist, and, carried away by his own celebrity, he turns out more work and thoroughly enjoys being fêted. Naturally enough, being a comedy, the story has a twist whereby the character's work gets mixed up with someone else's and he is soon exposed as a fake. Does it stop him painting? Absolutely not... and good for him!

Creative flow starts when we start it. If, for instance, you long in your heart to paint, then put some paint on paper. It doesn't matter whether you are 'good' or not in the eyes of others – the point is that you enjoy expressing your creativity. So have fun and let yourself go. Be an artist. Love it. Love everything about it – the paper or other medium you work on; the feel, colours and smell of paint; the brushes; the whole process. You can forget about the product – that's essentially unimportant, at least at this stage. What's important is the doing, the loving, the excitement, the fun and the sheer pleasure of it.

Don't worry if at first your loved ones are sceptical. Carry on regardless. Remember this is about you, your faith in yourself and your need to unlock your creativity. The more creative you are and the more you show it in your behaviour and self-faith, even if it's really put on, the more other people will believe your own publicity and, increasingly, think of you as a creative person. It's another circle – their interest and belief in you will feel good and give you an incentive to keep up your creativity and be the real thing – a highly creative person.

I'm not suggesting you pretend to be something you're not. You are naturally creative, and taking that further and letting your creative longing and ability flow by giving it a chance to show itself will enable it to develop. As the saying goes, 'Walk the talk and talk the walk!' As with your free-flow daily writing, the first step is to 'show up' on the page, the canvas, in your craft or in your work at the office – wherever your creativity needs to show itself, let it happen.

Boost your self-faith by creating a picture in your mind of how you would like your creativity to develop:

Try this
1 Take a few minutes to yourself. Sit quietly, breathe slowly and relax any tense muscles.
2 Imagine you are looking at a cinema screen.
3 Watch a clip of your life as you have been, seeing yourself on screen as someone who is unsure of your creativity.
4 Switch off this picture firmly.
5 See the blank screen. Keep breathing slowly. Relax some more.
6 Now switch on a new 'film'. In this one, you are self-assured, confident about your creativity, your ability and your work.
7 Feel how good it is to be confident and happy to be such a creative person.
8 See yourself in vivid colour and detail, living the creative life you wish to live.
9 Think of a particular scenario that, to you, is realistically possible and demonstrates your creativity, your ability and your happiness in living with it as a vibrant, wonderful, enjoyable part of your life.
10 Imagine it as though it's really happening, putting in as much detail as you wish. It's *you* in the film, your real life – you're there living it and loving it!
11 Think of a phrase that expresses these scenes in a nutshell. Remember it.
12 Think of a word that will instantly recall it for you. Remember it.
13 Know that the vision is yours to boost your faith in yourself, your creativity and your ability whenever you wish.
14 Understand that your subconscious will help you grow into the vision and live it for real.

'Imaging' is a powerful blend of imagining a scenario from the way of life you would like and showing your mind exactly what it's like. Once you have a clear image, it gives you something almost tangible to grow towards, like a plant reaching upwards for the light and warmth of the sun and downwards to the nutrients it needs. You will automatically do the same – reach out for whatever tools, experience, practice and help that will enable you to make yourself the version of you in the 'movie', and reach up to the inspiration and delight of using your creativity as you walk towards and into your vision.

Stuart, an IT expert, is a good example of someone who had a dream and made it real. He had a longing to express his creativity in a different genre. He wanted to be a fine-art photographer and make his living at it. He saved hard and in time managed to finance a two-year timeframe in which to pursue his ambition and see if he could make it work.

His website and stunning photographs were well received and he had a successful exhibition at a fine-art gallery. To generate a more regular income in between sales, he established himself as a top-of-the-market wedding photographer, using his IT skills to produce glossy books of the 'happy day' for his clients.

But at the end of the time he'd given himself to live his dream, he realized that professional photography was not what he wanted to do in the long term. While he loved the artistic side of his work and the pleasure his photos gave his clients, he missed the steadiness and the higher, more reliable income of his IT career. He also found that working on his own was not for him and realized he loved working in a team. He told me that he was hugely glad he'd lived his dream and would always enjoy photography, but in future it would be purely as a creative interest while he resumed working in the IT field.

How we explore our creativity is personal and, as it depends on so many variables, can be very flexible. And, through a lifetime, nothing is set in stone. Dreams may change before, during or after you realize them. All we can do – all we *need* to do – is live in the moment. By recognizing your creative longing, moving into it and being it, you will enjoy one of life's greatest pleasures, caring for your creativity. Remember this mantra:

Recognize it.

Respect it.

Let it live.

Help your creativity to flourish the way you long for it to, as long as it is meant to be.

Move with it, flexibly and fluently, whichever way you are meant to go.

> **Insight**
>
> Although we may have a good idea of how we would like our creativity to progress, we cannot know for sure how that will feel and where it will take us. Just as our feelings can change, so can the form of our creativity – it's a living, vibrant thing. But you do know how you feel *now* and, in recognizing your longing you began to set your creativity free. Dream your dream, step into it and rejoice.

Buffering and transforming others' negativity

The things people say! Everyone who is creative is likely to find their work attracts some negative comments. People, especially those close to us, often think it's their prerogative to say exactly what they think. Even those who are normally polite and sensitive and wouldn't dream, for instance, of saying something unkind about your appearance, may think it's fine to make cutting remarks about your creative work.

Over the years I've seen people abandon their creative passion in the wake of negative criticism. For example, my uncle was thrilled with the love and considerable natural flair he'd discovered for painting since he'd retired from business. He couldn't stop talking about what fun it was and I for one was very pleased about his new lease of life and enthusiasm. But next time I saw him he was strangely silent about it, and when I enquired how it was going, he said dismissively: 'Oh – someone in the group I belonged to kept telling me what was wrong with my work and how I should be doing it. I realized I was no good, so I've given up.' He had been so deeply hurt by the crassly insensitive 'advice' that none of us could persuade him to ignore it and resume the painting he'd so loved.

Another accomplished watercolourist whose work I loved gave up painting after attending a course where the tutor criticized her style and tried to make her change it. She, too, had been convinced she was 'no good at it.' Similarly, a client, Jill, gave up writing after a friend read her first novel and told her she didn't like the style. Though I thankfully managed to reignite her enthusiasm and flair for writing, she would write only non-fiction because her confidence as a fiction writer was irreparably damaged.

I would hate your creativity to be undermined like this, and beg you not to take it to heart if ever you're subjected to such slings and arrows. Remind yourself this: of course we make mistakes. Of course we can improve. But the fact is we are letting our creativity flow. We are *trying*. And we are having a great time doing so.

I'm writing this so that you are prepared for unsolicited and negative criticism and will know how to deflect it and refuse to be deterred from letting your creativity flow. Here are some ways to help:

- ▶ Imagine you're wearing a mental suit of armour so that any cutting comments bounce off you.
- ▶ Remember that personal opinions are subjective. Not everyone, for instance, will like your work but some people will love it.
- ▶ Reflect that people who are harshly critical would probably love to be as creative as you and are envious of your joy in your creativity.
- ▶ Say 'Blow them!' and carry on. A fabulous painter I know dropped out of college when the tutor insisted she change her technique and has gone on to find huge acclaim nonetheless.

The vital thing is that you love your creativity and are true to yourself and your dreams.

Another fun way to cope with criticism, especially the veiled kind, is to laugh about it and share the comments with friends who do appreciate your creativity. Here is a list of some I and fellow creative friends have collected and which we love to chuckle about when we get together:

Typical critical comments

General:

- ▶ 'You and your silly ideas!'
- ▶ 'Face it, sweetheart, you'll never be any good.'
- ▶ 'Don't give up the day job.'
- ▶ 'What makes you think you're so creative?'
- ▶ 'You can't call yourself an artist unless your work sells.'
- ▶ 'Why don't you save yourself the hassle and give up.'

Of paintings:

- ▶ 'Well, you wouldn't put it on your wall, would you?'
- ▶ 'Water is so difficult to paint, isn't it?'
- ▶ 'It would make nice wrapping paper.'
- ▶ 'Why don't you try other colours?'
- ▶ 'Why do you think it isn't working?'
- ▶ [delivered in a bored voice] 'Hmm, interesting.'
- ▶ And finally my favourite: 'Ooh… I *love* the frame!'

Learn immediately, if you receive a comment like these, not to ask this critic for an opinion in future – you simply can't trust them to care for your creative soul.

Insight

The best friends, teachers and mentors will appreciate your creativity and sensitivity and encourage you. They'll realize, too, that you are on a learning curve and will praise you generously for your effort and enthusiasm at this moment and your current ability. They are the ones to turn to for reassurance and encouragement to continue.

Learn to choose advisers and teachers whom you can trust to be objective in their assessment of your work and who know what they're talking about. They will also understand that personal opinions should only be given if they are positive, so if none is forthcoming don't press for one.

Remember that there are fashions in all creative work and, if your work doesn't happen to be on trend now, it doesn't mean that it isn't good or doesn't have potential. But more on this in Chapter 10.

When we're in the process of unlocking our creativity we need to take care of it and of ourselves. Above all:

- ▶ walk hand in hand with your creativity
- ▶ protect it fiercely and loyally.
- ▶ remember it's unique
- ▶ be glad it's part of you
- ▶ have faith in it
- ▶ cherish it with all your heart
- ▶ express it with joy!

6 POINTS OF REFLECTION

1 Conversation is a way for one soul to connect with another. Enjoy your rapport and notice how it sparks creative ideas and energy.

2 When you're with others, be a willing and enthusiastic team member or leader. Groups can generate an astonishingly high creative energy and you can be part of it.

3 If you have the good fortune to be in a creative partnership, cherish and nurture the goodwill between you and rejoice in how you inspire and harness each other's creativity.

4 Get some exercise with others – for all sorts of physiological and psychological reasons it's good for you and it gives your creativity a direct boost, too.

5 Alone or with others take joy in music, dancing and laughter and any kind of play – our creativity loves to have fun.

6 You can't stop others putting their negative oar in, but you can dodge or buffer the impact. Make sure you do and don't let them get to you.

8

The right-brain and left-brain effect on creativity

In this chapter you will learn about:
- *the way the brain works with our creativity*
- *the emotional/spiritual/imaginative/intuitive side*
- *the thoughtful/controlling/practical side*
- *the way they do a great job in tandem.*

The way the brain works with our creativity

When we sense and tap into our creativity we use our brains in different ways: it's partly an intuitive and emotional process and partly a matter of reasoning and practical or academic expertise. All these work together in a complex and fascinating way that scientists continue to research and are discovering more and more about all the time.

It is, of course, an extremely complex subject area but fortunately we don't need in-depth scientific knowledge to understand how we can encourage our brains to let our creativity flow. But understanding just a little about the way our brains affect our creativity is hugely helpful in recognizing its scope and using it.

So often our schooling and early experience leads us to the conviction we can't do something creative we've tried, such as drawing or singing for example. When I was a child, I thought I couldn't draw. I longed to be able to draw horses and other animals because I loved them so, and I tried and tried, but each time I had a go the result would be out of proportion and not much like the animal at all. However hard I tried to copy a photo or the form of a living animal in front of me, it didn't make the drawing any better – in fact, the harder I tried, the worse it got.

I knew in my bones that I was very creative, but feared I didn't have the talent or expertise to use it as I'd like to. In time, I had the good fortune to work for someone who encouraged my love of writing and helped me gain professional experience and make it my career. Then, out of the blue and thanks again to a mentor, this one an artist, I discovered the magic of paint and colour and found I could paint pictures expressing my individuality in the style of the ones I longed to have in my house but couldn't afford – Kandinsky, Monet, Van Gogh, Matisse, Marsden Hartley. With these artists as my inspiration I had (and still have) a whale of a time painting pictures I loved and which look terrific on my walls. To my delight, I found that others sometimes like them, too.

It felt like a miracle. The girl who couldn't draw still couldn't as a mature woman, but I *could* paint. And then came another miracle: I discovered, thanks to the writer Betty Edwards and her book *Drawing on the Right Side of Your Brain*, that I could draw, too. (See 'Taking it further' at the end of this book for publication details.) I vividly remember doing the first exercise I tried from the book. If you think you can't draw, try this similar one now. Even if you're not interested in drawing as such, you'll be intrigued to see how well your brain copes when you look at something from a different perspective.

Try this
1 Take a photograph – of a man or woman sitting on a chair that has four legs and a back.
2 Register how you feel at the thought of drawing it. (I remember thinking, for instance, 'That's ridiculous, I couldn't possibly draw that!')
3 Turn the picture upside down.
4 Don't be fazed by the fact you've never seen such a strange-looking image before – that's the whole point!
5 Forget all about it being an upside-down man or woman sitting on an upside-down chair and simply see it as some lines you want to copy.
6 Take a pencil or pen and draw what you see without trying to make sense of the peculiar form in front of you. As far as

possible, keep your hand moving continuously. Just put down
what you see.

7 Keep going until you've finished drawing the whole image.

8 Now turn your drawing upside down.

You'll find you've drawn, quite competently, a good, recognizable
likeness of a person sitting on a chair.

I was gobsmacked, as I expect you are if you've just finished your
drawing. I knew all too well that if I'd tried to draw the figure on
the chair the right way up I wouldn't have succeeded. I realized
in that moment that, if those of us who normally find drawing
difficult take out of the equation the area of the brain that thinks
logically, we can far more easily replicate an image on paper. In
other words, if we can use our eyes and a pencil, and let go of
assumptions about what something looks like, we can *all* draw.
All we need to do – and this applies to so many creative things – is
let go of our preconceptions and go by what we actually see or
subconsciously know.

Equally exciting is that, once you understand that you can 'draw with
the right side of your brain', you can use the confidence this gives you
to work with the more analytical side, too. These days, if I set my
mind to it and let my intuitive and logical sides work in tandem, I can
usually make a fair stab at drawing well.

The first person to discover that different parts of the brain tend
to influence different abilities was the French physician Pierre Paul
Broca in 1861. More definitive evidence came from studies carried
out in the 1960s by the American neuropsychologist Roger Sperry
and his colleagues. Since then, it's become generally assumed that
the left hemisphere of the frontal cortex is associated with verbal and
reasoning function, and the right hemisphere with artistic, intuitive
and spatial ability.

However, it isn't quite as simple and clear-cut as this. The brain is
extraordinarily complex and the various parts work together, helping
each other out and harmonizing in often beautiful synchronicity. This
is a boon to the process of unlocking our creativity and letting it flow
because so much of it involves a visual or visionary ability coupled
with organizational or technical skills.

I will still occasionally find I just can't draw something, and experience again the frustration I felt as a child. Nowadays, though, by recalling how different areas of the brain affect the way we function creatively, I can usually unlock my ability by switching the way I work to a more visual, intuitive mode. Then, suddenly, a drawing I'm pleased with will appear. It's as though my fingers work independently of me with a life and vision of their own.

The more we practise using together the visual/intuitive and logical/ analytical parts of our brain, the easier it becomes to draw or produce other creative work to order. Both are equally valid ways in their own right to enable your creativity and the kind of ratio in which you dovetail them will depend on the particular form of creativity you're using at the time. Scientists, for example, are often as creative as artists, but they will tend to work from an analytical foundation, bringing in imagination and intuition to stimulate innovative thinking, while an artist will probably work the other way around.

Insight

As a creative person, is it better to use the intuitive side of your brain more? Not necessarily. It depends on you – the way you like to work, and the way you use the various facets of your creativity. What all creative people right across the scientific–artistic spectrum have in common is that we love to use our imagination and/or ingenuity in coming up with an original way of approaching an idea or project. And when we're in touch with both 'sides of our brain' as our creativity flows, it's a fantastic feeling of wholeness and fulfilment. Magic? No – but it feels like it!

Our emotional/spiritual/imaginative/intuitive side

Almost certainly, however, when our creativity is blocked or we feel unimaginative and blinkered, it's because we're being too logical. The way to free ourselves and let our creative energy flow again is by practising going into what I'll call 'right-brain mode'. It's surprisingly easy to do so at will whenever you wish.

Meditation, or an exercise in 'assumption-less' drawing like the upside-down chair one, or any one of the other exercises or reflections throughout this book – all can invite your brain to free up your creativity and let you feel utterly connected and at one with it. It's about feeling, sensing and loving the prospect of being creative.

It's about letting yourself be aware of what you're itching or aching to do. It could come to you in many ways:

▶ Sometimes a recognition or deepened understanding of this will come when you're deep in contemplation or simply sitting quietly and 'listening' for inspiration.
▶ A guided visualization can be cathartic in showing us the creative way ahead.
▶ Creative insight might come as a response to prayer.
▶ It could be that you randomly come across a sudden sense of creative purpose.
▶ Perhaps you'll be overwhelmed with the beauty all around you, or in one particular facet of your life or the world, and this will be all it takes to awaken your creativity and start planning or producing something beautiful in response.
▶ Alternatively, you might be deeply moved by something you hear in the news or learn about in your own family or community and need to let the emotion flow into a creative project.
▶ It could be a holistic bringing-together of some or all of these things.

We'll be looking in depth at meditation and spiritual and mystical creativity-freeing practices in Chapter 9. But meanwhile you can get into the habit of sensing creative longings and surges and taking in any rational thoughts or intuitive ideas you have on expressing them. Practise letting your creative feelings flow by:

▶ remembering to write your daily free-flow pages
▶ appreciating the astonishing complexity of the world and reflecting on, or – if you're not a believer – imagining, its creator. Think about the intelligence he/she/it must have had to create this world and the infinite universe beyond.

Now imagine, instead, the mind-blowing blend of serendipity and order that, if there were *no* creator, would have come haphazardly out of the nothing or the chaos that preceded our universe:

1 Let your thoughts and any accompanying feelings flow as you ponder the creation of our world, however it came about.
2 Sense the creative energy flowing through you in response.
3 Pause. Feel it. Feel the wonder.

You are now using the right side of your brain. Register the feeling and know that you can return to it at will when you wish and that it will become easier to make the switch the more familiar you become with the feeling.

It's a feeling like no other when creativity flows intuitively and emotionally or as an almost visceral gut feeling. It's also wonderful when this flow expresses itself in a technical way, as in Stephen's case below.

Stephen is paid a retainer to generate ideas for an IT software company. I was intrigued by the way he integrated his creative flair with his knowledge of IT. This is the interview he kindly gave me:

J: How do you come up with ideas?

S: I don't know. They arrive.

J: Do you have any techniques or practices to encourage them to?

S: Not really. I suppose I keep an eye – or should that be an ear – open for them all the time though.

J: And they pop into your mind out of the blue?

S: Yes, very often.

J: As a fully fledged idea?

S: It's wonderful when that happens – and it has once or twice. But usually I'll get an element of an idea and work on it.

J: What does that involve?

S: I usually register it and think 'Hmm – wonder if there's something in that.' Then I'll let it hang about around me – not exactly in the back of my mind, it's really as though it's all around me somehow – for as long as it wants. One day it comes together.

J: So you don't consciously fret about it, or try and pin it down too quickly?

S: I don't at all. It feels like an entity in itself that will be born when it's ready. That sounds horribly pretentious, sorry, but that's truly how it feels. Once it's ready, then it's a case of getting to work on how it can be implemented – a prototype design perhaps and always an outline of what it's for and why it will be popular. If I have the knowledge to do it, I add a few basic notes on how it will work. But what I'm essentially commissioned to do is the imaginative part. I don't need to get involved with the technical side because, if the company like the proposal, they'll put their design and production teams onto it.

J: Does it feel like your product – your baby?

S: Absolutely. But when it's time to let go, it's time to let go – like when your children grow up and fly the nest. Not as major as that obviously – but, yes, it is like letting your baby go.

J: And how does it feel, through this whole cycle?

S: Exciting sometimes. Extremely satisfying as it comes together as a viable proposal. Ultimately very fulfilling. I just love it.

J: A feeling of flow?

S: That's what creativity is, isn't it? Letting it flow, expressing that creative impulse and energy inside you.

J: What do you do when an idea is – what would you call it – germinating? Do you work at other things?

S: Yes, of course I do – I'd get bored hanging about waiting around as one project develops. I work at other things – some creative, some physical and practical. Actually the practical jobs often seem to cradle – or if you like incubate – the ideas.

J: Ah – that's interesting – do you think the practical side of you, the left side of your brain, is helpful to creativity?

S: I suppose it is. The two aspects of my work certainly seem to work well side by side.

J: Is there any way you can encourage the next idea to form?

S: Expectancy is the word that comes to mind. I have a more or less permanent feeling of anticipation.

J: Could that be useful advice to other creative people?

S: Yes – I think everyone can do that – anticipate ideas and inspiration coming through to them. And – and this is vital – noticing them when they do and paying attention. I've had ideas I've forgotten and never been able to recall. Now I pay attention to them immediately, welcome them and – sounds silly but there you go – love them, right from the start. I jot them down, too – just a word is all it takes to make sure you remember. We all need to pay attention because creativity is the most fantastic gift. Priceless. I'll never stop being grateful.

....

Insight

Ideas and creative insights may, as Stephen finds, appear in our minds at any moment. You may have asked for them or knowingly need them for your work, as he does, or they may be completely unsolicited. Enjoy their arrival and their presence and be ready for your creativity to flow as and when it's time.

....

Emotions are often a conduit for our creativity. In yet another kind of alchemy, we can let the emotion we feel play itself out in a burst or stream of creativity. A friend emailed me, full of joy at the beauty of the roadside verges in her area. The foxgloves, tall daisies and poppies were, she wrote, more beautiful than anything we could imagine, let alone create ourselves. I replied to her, truly empathizing with her joy as I thought immediately of the banks of foxgloves glowing in the sun that I'd passed on a recent walk. As I was writing the email, the first line of a poem popped into my mind and I wrote it there and then in one of those unbidden, instant creativity trips that, sometimes, an intense emotion enables.

We are often especially creative when we are feeling joyous – and often being creative make us feel joyous – it's very much a two-way thing. It's as though the energy bubbles over and expresses itself in work or delight.

Loss, trauma and anguish can all, in overwhelming us, cause such a maelstrom of sadness that again, but now in a heart-rending way, it overflows as creativity. This flow of creative energy can be healing and at the very least helps us to bear the pain that we are living through. It is always therapeutic if we allow it to be.

Anger is hugely powerful emotionally and by expressing it through our creativity we can defuse it and, often, transform it into something positive. Fear is another negative emotion where creativity can be therapeutic in helping us understand the causes. We can then, again with the help of a creative approach, convert it into a positive way of coping and moving constructively forward.

Is our sexuality a right- or left-brain expression? It may be either or both, depending on your attitude to it and the way you express it. Sex may be a purely or mostly physical activity, which may or may not give pleasure and the resulting release of feel-good hormones. Or it may be transformed by love, affection and care into a sublime all-round experience of physical, emotional and perhaps even spiritual pleasure and joy. It's also enhanced by a good knowledge of technique and an understanding of each other's individual preferences and responses. So, at its best, sex is a creative experience and a work of art in its own right. And, again, the emotions involved can be so powerful that they flow through us causing a tremendous wave of creative inspiration – as so many of our greatest writers, painters and other artists have shown in their beautiful erotic or sensual work.

Love is also, in all its many forms, a wonderful pathway that often leads to soaring or quietly purring creative energy, inspiration and expression.

In your creative expression, your emotions can be your friend and ally. When you let them flow they will fire your work, endowing it with a passion, energy and feeling that radiate outwards to others as well as back to yourself, both as you work and later when you review it. When we allow our emotion to accompany and infuse our creativity we often learn about ourselves, too. We'll look more at how this works and how it helps us in Chapter 10.

For now, take a few moments to reflect on the way emotion has influenced your creativity and how it could do so more in future:

Try this
1 Sit quietly and relax all your muscles.
2 Feel any tension leaving you as you do so.

3 One by one, consider the emotions in your life, including happiness, feelings of loss, sorrow, sexual or sensual desire and the associated feelings, anger, fear and love.

4 Write each emotion on a piece of paper and think how you would express it if you were making a creative work. For instance, how do you think you would or could paint, write or sculpt it? Or in what other creative ways could you express it? it.

5 When you've made your list, without thinking too much about the choice, decide on one or two that you will express through your creativity.

6 Mark your choice to remind you when you begin the project. In noting it in this way, you'll also set your subconscious on the path to becoming familiar with the idea in readiness for when you start.

When you have more free time you can start on your choice:

▶ Set aside a reasonable amount of time to create the work you have in mind or, if it's something like a journey or business idea that you can't put into action at this stage of your life, write about it fully or express it in paint or another medium of your choice.

▶ As you work, feel – or, if no feeling comes to mind, imagine you feel – your creative energy coursing through you, carrying the emotion you're expressing. Let it flow through your fingers or actions into the work.

▶ Remember there is no right or wrong way of doing this – it's a totally individual experience of letting emotion flow through your creativity.

▶ Take care of yourself as you work, remembering to eat and drink and, if you feel tired, to rest for a while to restore your energy.

▶ When you've finished or done as much as you wish for now, leave the work, relax and again take care of yourself, perhaps going for a walk with a friend or watching a television programme you enjoy and having a hot drink.

▶ All you need to do now is register the satisfaction of having let your creativity flow with the emotion(s) you chose. You can reflect on the exercise and what it meant to you tomorrow.

Insight

We are all naturally emotional creatures, yet as we go through life we learn to moderate the way we express our feelings to fit in with our family, friends and everyone with whom we come into contact. It may feel strange at first to loosen your hold on your emotions, but once you let go of them as they flow into and through your creative work, you'll probably find you release tension you may not have realized you harboured.

Our thoughtful/controlling/practical side

Verbal, academic and logistical skills, planning and organizing – all these are thought to be the provenance of the left side of the brain. In this mode, you use fact rather than imagination and so we tend to think of professionals working in science, medicine, teaching and the law as predominantly using left-brain abilities. This doesn't mean they're not creative – indeed, their creativity will undoubtedly enhance their expertise and success. Doctors, for instance, use their creativity to think of the best path to take them through the myriad of treatment options as they decide what will be best for the individual patient. Detectives have to work creatively as they plan investigations and searches.

All of us use the left side of our brain creatively in diverse and often complex ways as we manage and move through daily life. Assembling facts and organizing them into viable routes that suit all the people with whom we come into contact in the course of a day – all this takes enormous reserves of creativity.

So never let it be said of even the most meticulously organized person that they are not creative. Even if they're unaware of it, they are. And the same person – who probably claims not to be creative at all – can unlock their unused creativity in just the same way that a person who knows they are creative but feels blocked can. Both kinds of people will find it fun as they free their creativity and start to explore it and let it flow.

Insight

However biased we are in favour of academic, verbal and organizational abilities, our creativity probably still shines, or at least functions, through our lives and work, even when we have no idea we're being creative. And just as naturally artistic, imaginative and intuitive people can free up their creativity, so can those who consider themselves as firmly operating out of the left side of the brain recognize their existing creativity and tap unused reserves.

The way the right and left sides of our brain do a great job in tandem

It's funny how so many of us are quick to label ourselves. I've always thought of myself as being predominantly artistic or, in right/left brain terms, decidedly right-brain. But when I did a test recently to determine which dominates me, to my surprise my ratio was given as 54/46 in favour of right-brain.

When I thought it through, I realized that I do use the left side of my brain almost all the time. Much of my writing is based on years of study and experience and it's only when I go into a stream of consciousness – for instance, when I write poems or my free-flow pages – that I use my imaginative, intuitive side. Abstract painting is right-side; figurative drawing both left and right; colourful impressions are mostly right-brain but usually have some left-brain input, too.

It's also interesting to reflect that the power of thought and reason, which is often assumed to be a left-brain activity, can also be used to guide both our emotions and our creativity. In my book *Think Love* (Vega Books, 2002), I wrote about the way thought can bring love into everything we do, helping us behave well and often lighting up our lives in so many ways. In much the same way, thought can help us to get in touch with our creativity, unlock it and let it flow.

By using our brains to think of possible ways both to be creative and to free our creativity, we create a focus for what we want to do and how we can bring it into being. With thought we can also work out how to summon and develop the necessary energy, ability and experience.

Insight

Thought prompted you to read this book and will guide your choice of those sections that you particularly like and which will be most useful to your own unique mix of creativity. Your wonderful, extraordinarily complex brain is your ally and your partner in creativity. Treasure it and let it help you. It is your greatest asset and an astonishingly valuable gift.

6 POINTS OF REFLECTION

1 Your brain knows every aspect of your creativity – how it's working now, its potential, the best ways to help it flow – everything. Think, listen and feel and you'll be able to look after your creativity well.

2 Are you a right-brain or left-brain kind of person? Do the different areas of the brain affect your creativity? It's a fascinating question and your creativity will enjoy exploring it.

3 Reflect on how your 'right-brain' side may embrace emotional, spiritual and imaginative aspects and perhaps let your creativity flow easily, too.

4 Then think about the 'left-brain' characteristics – the ones that plan and organize and enable you to have self-discipline and get things done.

5 Can you feel the way all of these aspects of you and your creativity interact and work together?

6 Practise moving from one set of abilities to the other and see if you feel more at home on one 'side' of your brain than the other. Either way, both sides will still work together – feel how good it is to know that!

9

Mystical ways to let your creativity come through

In this chapter you will learn about:
- *the way imagination influences our creativity*
- *the usefulness of boredom*
- *meditation*
- *developing a feeling of connection with the creative essence of the world and the universe.*

> Listening for inspiration
>
> Listening,
>
> We keen to the voice divine
>
> Loosening
>
> The stays that bind us down
>
> Free,
>
> We move towards our destiny.

The way imagination influences our creativity

We all have the ability to conjure up in our minds aspects of life we have previously experienced including thoughts and sensual impressions. We can see and feel them all over again 'in our mind's eye'. Taking this a stage further, imagination also includes the way we can 'live' in our mind things we haven't actually experienced but for which we create images and other sensory impressions.

Imagination helps us understand the mass of information we take in and enables us to empathize or sympathize with others. It helps us make sense of the world, learn and use our knowledge in all kinds of ways. It helps us think 'What if?', letting our minds run on and explore different paths and even realms. Imagination is a vital key to using our creativity, loving it passionately and enjoying it to the full, and it's a wonderful resource that's open to us all.

In the same way that many people claim they're not creative, many deny having imagination. They do – it's just that perhaps they don't realize how much they use it, or that they may have lost the knack of recognizing and using it. But we can all practise using imagination to help our creativity flow… and it feels good in itself, too.

How to let your imagination live and soar

When we are children, our imagination is natural to us. Given the chance we play in situations and worlds of our own making, and have a literally fantastic time. It helps us develop generally and use our minds creatively and thoughtfully. It helps us have fun and relish the joy and other emotions of life. It helps make every day an adventure, full of happiness and excitement.

For this reason, we need to be careful not to fill every moment of our children's lives with organized activity. Kids benefit hugely from plenty of time to daydream and let their imagination stretch out and run free. But so do adults. If you fill your life with work, things to do, places to go, people to see and never have any time to be idle and let your mind roam free, your imagination won't have the chance to explore either and, along with your creativity, will probably go to sleep.

It's perfectly possible to provide yourself with the ideal conditions to encourage and nurture your imagination and, simultaneously, your creativity. They are:

1 SOME TIME TO YOURSELF

Once again, I can't stress enough how vital this is. If you're always with others and/or always working or otherwise occupied, your imagination won't have a chance to thrive. It probably won't even have the chance to venture out, and, if it does, you'll probably be too busy to notice it, or will consider it tiresome and push it under again. Let your new mantra be: 'Make time and take time to let your imagination thrive.' Give it some space – it needs it. *You* need it.

If I had a pound for every time I was pulled back from a flight of my imagination at school with words such as 'Stop daydreaming!' or 'Concentrate!' or as an adult by phrases like 'Where are you?', 'Hello? ! Come back to us!', 'What are you thinking about?', 'Don't go to sleep!' and 'Are you asleep?' I'd be rich!

Of course, they may often have a point because we need to concentrate at work or when we're busy with something at home. And it's hugely important to pay loving, interested attention to our loved ones. But in your leisure hours you also need time to dream, and you should help your family and friends understand the importance of letting you have peace and quiet to do this. So, if you say you want ten minutes' silence, they should respect your wish and know not to interrupt. Same if you shut your eyes, whether or not you are going to sleep. These days I am very firm about this. If someone does interrupt a meditation or snooze, I ask them not to do so again – unless, obviously, there is an emergency.

The good thing for you and everyone about having dedicated imagination time is that in a few minutes you'll accomplish a lot in terms of free-flow thought, imaging and 'listening for' creative ideas. Perhaps, on occasion, nothing like that will come, but that's fine, too, as at least you'll have a lovely few minutes of total mind relaxation. Either way you will 'come back' to everyone refreshed and invigorated.

Knowing you've given your imagination and creativity a chance to flow makes you feel really good. So, as well as explaining to your family why you need to take a patch of time for yourself, be sure to reward them for their understanding by afterwards focusing on them. Then they'll see your quiet time as a good thing for them as well and, instead of sabotaging it, make sure you have it. I find that, once introduced to the idea of a personal quiet time, others want to try it out for themselves and usually love it so much they, too, will make it a daily or at least regular treat.

2 A WILLINGNESS AND EAGERNESS TO DREAM

Attitude is as important to our imaginative, creative soul as any other aspect of life. If we approach the idea of providing ourselves with the ideal conditions to dream with negativity or grumpy reluctance, we probably won't create them. Positivity and pleasure are vital to the right ambience. My analogy is with a nest that's lined with the softest material where, as though floating in water, I can completely forget my body and let my mind go wandering, allowing it to relax deeply and blissfully. It's a place where I go with a sense of love and warmth, peace and relaxation, and yet a delightful feeling of expectation, too.

Try this
Find your own special imagining place:

1 Pause for a few moments.
2 As usual, relax any tense muscles.
3 Breathe slowly.
4 Now consider what would be the perfect place to enjoy some quiet time to relax and free your imagination.
5 Imagine you are there.
6 How does it feel?
7 Remember everything you like about it.

Know that, whenever you visit this place to rest, you will relax completely and feel safe to let your imagination roam and creative ideas come to you.

Let's hear it for ambling and idling, too. There is a time for soaring and striding, being dynamic and focused, perhaps even relentlessly and intensely striving. But equally important – for some more so – is the ability to relax and potter, letting our thoughts meander where they will. In such calm timelessness when your spirit is at rest, you may discover or plant some seeds of creativity.

The usefulness of boredom

Boredom has a bad press. It tends to be seen as something we don't want to tolerate in our lives. There are sayings like 'If you're bored with London you're bored with life' and 'If you're bored, you're boring.'

There's certainly no need to be bored in London or, indeed, wherever we are. Modern life offers endless possibilities for interesting pursuits. And it's easy and feels good to take an interest in lots of things and in other people. But a certain amount of boredom can be great as far as creativity is concerned and I've learned to welcome it as an invitation to go into the quiet space for inspiration, or to think what's behind the feeling of boredom and remedy it.

Again, we have only to look at children's behaviour when they're feeling bored to see how useful it can be in inducing creativity. Kids will moan they're bored and, usually, their parents try as hard as they can to come up with things to occupy them. But leave them be and they will eventually invent their own games, using their creativity, or start to daydream, creating new, fantastic worlds into which they step. All this stretches and develops their imagination and creativity.

Boredom can do the same for us. Try this exercise next time you are bored:

Try this
1 Register the feeling of boredom and focus on it.
2 How does it feel? Notice the emotions surround it and where they are manifested in your body? For instance, you might feel tight across your shoulders, or the muscles around your mouth might be compressed.
3 Relax the area affected, consciously dropping the tension.
4 Consider how you can now similarly assuage the feeling of boredom from your mind.
5 Take a while to think what you would really, really like to do.
6 Let your imagination take you where it wishes.
7 Afterwards reflect on whether any of these wishes could be realistic in your life with some creative thought, together with planning and determination.

Remember that even when what you've imagined is unrealistic for whatever reason in your life now, you can make use of it in another way for good and enjoyment. Think sideways – again letting your creativity and imagination work out a good route forward for you.

When I carry out this exercise, I usually get a clear impression of what I need to be doing. By 'need' I mean what my soul is longing for me to do. It could be just something that will obliquely but nevertheless surely encourage my creativity such as going for a walk in a park, the countryside or by the sea. Or it could be a way I can be instantly creative such as painting a picture or writing a poem.

When I've done this session with others, they've come up with all kinds of ways of moving forward creatively – from making notes for an impending business meeting to not just vaguely wishing they could have another home but sitting down to create a floor plan incorporating all the things they'd like in it. As soon as we realize what we can do, a feeling of excitement or pleasure moves in to replace the stultifying boredom. Instead of feeling tense and uncomfortable, notice how alert your mind and body feel, ready to support you in whatever you're planning to do.

At this stage, you may like to put on some music that you love – it will lift your spirits even higher and carry you forwards in your new mission. Above all – don't put off what you've planned to do. If possible, start on it immediately; if you can't, put aside a definite time for it as soon as possible.

Insight

Rather than letting boredom drag us down into an irritating state of inertia, we can coax it along until it turns into something else – a state of contemplative expectancy. There you can go wherever your imagination wants to, noticing and paying attention to any ideas and visions that come to you along the way. In the process, the negative feelings of being bored will be zapped and in will come a great feeling of positivity and new purpose. The state of boredom will thus be transformed into a seedbed for your creativity.

Just this morning on the radio, a best-selling novelist said that, when her previous employer, a television company, failed to renew her contract, she daydreamed that one day, when she'd made it as a novelist, they would ask her to return, now with a full appreciation of her ability. Her dream came true. Does having a dream somehow draw it to us in our real life? It certainly sometimes feels like that and I keep an open mind on the subject. What is definitely true is that when we have a dream it focuses the mind and we can, with dedication, planning and effort, move towards making it real.

Meditation

Meditation is another state of relaxation which often enables us to gain a profound awareness of our creative wishes and inspiration. Even if we don't meditate expressly for this purpose, creative ideas often nonetheless seem to come to us during the session, or, facilitated by it, arrive later. There are several ways this happens:

▶ The oasis of peace allows us to soothe anxious thoughts and confusion. In enjoying a respite from life's stresses, we enable our subconscious to explore creative possibilities for us.

▶ During meditation we are in close contact with our intuition and through it may sense solutions to questions about our current creative projects. We may also see clearly the creative path forward.

▶ It may also be creatively rich in possibility because it enables a spiritual connection, but more about this in the next section.

You can meditate while doing something else that frees your mind; for instance, I recently talked with a long-distance runner who meditated as he trained. But most of us, especially early on as we get used to the practice, like to sit or walk at a leisurely pace. You don't need a special place for meditation – although the familiar routine of settling down in one helps us very quickly or even instantly to relax. For this reason, it's good to choose the same place when you're at home, but you can meditate anywhere where you can 'switch off' for a few minutes – for instance, when travelling as a car, train or aeroplane passenger.

People often worry that they won't be able to stop obsessing about what's going on in their life, but it's surprising how quickly we learn to empty our minds of busy thoughts and worries, or simply to let thoughts come and go without dwelling on them. Should anything persist in worrying you, say to yourself that you will address it later, after the meditation, as for now you are at peace and recharging your batteries.

There are many ways to enter a meditative state. You may, for instance, like to use a mantra – a word whose meaning and sound you like. Simply keep repeating it to yourself. My meditation friends usually opt to use a guided visualization. Sometimes one of us will talk us through one of our favourites, like the example below, or we may listen to one on a CD. Some prefer to have gentle, pleasant but essentially undemanding music as a background. Once you get used to meditating, you may find you prefer to go straight into meditation without the need for any preamble. There are many ways and all that matters is that you follow one that feels comfortable.

Here are two practical points:

1 *Is meditation best done alone or with others?*
Either are fine as long as any others are committed to stillness and quietness, whether they are taking part in the meditation or not. For most people it would be difficult, if not impossible, to meditate with someone who is restless or who is mischievously making fun of you.

2 *What position is best?*
Choose a position comfortable for you so you can relax physically with no pressure on any part of the body to disturb you. If you are very supple, the classic position is cross-legged on the floor. It's fine to be sitting in a chair where your spine will be straight and your feet on the floor. Kneeling is good, too, with a cushion under your bum so that you can sit back on your heels and, again, easily keep your back straight. In the daytime, flat on your back is another good position – but if you are tired you'll almost certainly fall asleep, in which case choose another position.

Here are some suggestions for a way of meditating that encourages creativity:

▶ **When you're ready to meditate…** relax every part of you. Some like to do this in sequence from toes to head. Feel your muscles unclenching – so often we tense them unknowingly. Feel all the tension flowing out of your body and let the chair or the floor take all your weight as you relax.

▶ **Let go of all your thoughts and emotions** – Now have a sense of clearing your mind of worries and letting go emotionally.

▶ **And forgive** – Now forgive anyone who you feel has wronged or upset you, in the past or very recently. This will stop negative emotion blocking your creativity. Let any negative feelings fade away.

▶ **Shut your eyes or choose your focus** – I meditate with my eyes closed; others prefer to let their gaze rest on something like the flame of a candle.

▶ **Follow *your* way** – Use your preferred way, as mentioned above, to go into a meditative state. You may like to try my favourite path. It's similar to a route used for self-hypnosis but instead of going down into your inner being you are going upwards to something beyond and greater than yourself in search of calm and completeness and as a conduit to and for your creativity. Another time, if you like, you can create a visualization of your own to follow.

Here is one of our favourite visualizations:

1 Take your time on this imaginary journey, pausing between the various stages to take in all you are sensing and enjoy the feeling of peace. You and any others you are leading in this visualization can then fill in your own personally imagined details about the path and everything you see and sense.

2 Imagine you are walking up steps. Concentrate on each step, feeling it beneath your feet. After a while, you will see that you're coming to the top of the flight of steps. Now step onto the grassy path you've reached. Walk up its gentle incline, imagining your favourite flowers growing on either side and their scent drifting over you, meeting the smell of the grass beneath your feet. After a hundred yards or so, the path opens out and you see you are coming out onto a grassy cliff top with a wonderful view of the ocean and sky. An imaginary wiseperson, in whom you immediately have utter, complete trust, is sitting waiting for you. A sense of safety, warmth, love and welcome suffuses you and you sit down in their company to enjoy the utter peace. You are totally relaxed, not thinking of anything. All is well. You have a sense of being supported by the peace all around you.

3 Now simply rest in their company. You are totally calm, and have no thoughts; there is pure concentration on being and nothing else. Be aware of purity, peace, love and joy. You may like to ask for guidance if you are at a creative crossroads or uncertain time. Don't expect to be given an instant answer or solution. Often guidance comes at some stage afterwards and it can take time for the right answer or way forward to be illuminated for you. For now just enjoy the stillness.

4 However long you have set aside to meditate, you will know when the time is right to stop and come back to your day-to-day world. Before you leave your companion they will give you a gift that symbolizes a helpful gift you already have in your life. Don't worry if you don't realize its significance straight away; it will come to you within a day or two.

5 Say thank you and leave, retracing your steps until you are home again. Take in the sense of fulfilment, calm and peace. You may like to continue meditating silently amid this lovely feeling of calm for a few minutes more.

Insight

As we become used to meditating, the easier it is to let go of everyday concerns and slip into an oasis of peace and creative openness. And you'll find that the more often you meditate, the more often you'll want to do it. Ideally, aim to meditate every day – it makes such a difference to us and to our flow of creativity when we do this. After a while you'll find you can meditate anywhere and anytime you have a few minutes of inactivity to spare alone.

Meditation is good for our creativity whichever way we do it. Following a visualization like the one above can release creative inspiration and the vibrant energy to act on it. Sometimes it's a fully fledged idea; sometimes a dawning sense of the creative path you would like to follow. If ever I'm feeling blocked or unsure, it's usually during a time when I've let regular meditation lapse. So the first thing I do is set aside some time for a meditation. It's always cathartic in unblocking my creative flow and it feels good in mind, body and spirit, too.

Spirit? Yes, very much so – let's take a look at this now and see how soulful connection with something beyond our understanding often has a huge impact on our creativity.

Developing a spiritual feeling of connection with the creative essence of the world and the universe

Many of our painters, musicians and other artists – and creative people of all kinds – have spoken of their feeling that their creativity is a gift from a dimension beyond the confines of our lives and world. Whether they believe in, and speak of it as, God, or are atheists or agnostics, they feel strongly that there is a spiritual element belonging either to our world or beyond it from which they draw creative inspiration and sustenance.

We all have our own opinions on whether or not there is a creator, but most of us agree that there can be a mystical feeling of connection when our creative purpose and work seem to arrive from another place completely beyond our control. We feel at one with this connection and the creativity that flows through us. It feels as if there is an extraordinary, powerful link between our spirituality and creativity and us. As they complement each other, it is as though they create an incredible synchronicity and fire us up creatively. Ideas come like blessings in the wind and everything falls into place as we make plans, work and bring the project to fruition.

This inexplicable providence may be experienced by everyone creative, in all kinds of work, walks of life and types of creativity. Many successful businesspeople, for instance, have experienced it and describe it as a wave of inspiration and energy propelling the project forward.

We can work and try and push and pull – and get nowhere. Then this wonderful synergy comes along and, not necessarily effortlessly, but in a sense easily and graciously, the work seamlessly moves forward to completion.

Judith, an entrepreneur and talented artist, told me this has often happened to her and described her impression of the dynamic energy she felt, what it meant to her and how it felt:

'I call it being in flow. There have been many times when I've struggled with projects – it could be a business development or a sculpture, for instance – perhaps for days or even months. Sometimes I've been on the point of giving up because I felt so frustrated at it not working. And then all of a sudden things change. Like a jigsaw, the pieces that I couldn't put in place before, no matter how hard I tried, spontaneously sort themselves out and slot into place. All my endeavour couldn't make it happen, but then it's as though something else, something outside of us, moves in and helps us bring it about.'

She smiled as she reflected on such times, her face lighting up: 'It's not that you stop working – but the effort and work stop being difficult and the energy just comes to you. It's a feeling that you and the project are working in total harmony with whatever it is – this outside helper. Sounds loopy, probably, but it's like you're at one with the universe, somehow, and everything is possible. Sometimes I look back at what I've done and think "How on earth did I do it?" I can't imagine being able to do something like that now, having that flow of energy and synchronicity. But hopefully I will, with other projects. God willing.' She smiled ruefully this time and added: 'I don't actually believe in religion. But perhaps there is some kind of energy in another dimension – I don't know, who does? – that somehow we connect with...'

Judith has described very eloquently the phenomenon of flow many creative people experience and which some believe is the result of divine providence. Whatever it is exactly and however it works, it does happen. By continuing to exercise our creativity as well as we can, we invite it into our lives. When it comes, rejoice and relish it.

> Try this
> Think now of any times in your life when things have worked well for you and you've felt in harmony with your purpose and work:
>
> 1 Jot down some notes about what happened.
> 2 Take a moment to relive your feelings at the time when everything came right.
> 3 Notice how you are feeling now as you remember this time of 'flow'.
> 4 Describe how it felt again, jotting it down.
> 5 If you like, paint a picture or in another way make something to express what happened and your feelings about it, then and now.
> 6 Think of it as a celebration of the gift of synchronicity you received.
> 7 Keep it, or if it's something perishable like landscape art or a celebration cake, take a photo of it, as a memento of your experience and as a future inspiration.

Listening for inspiration

Be alert to anything interesting for your creative pulse. We get
creative ideas and inspiration in so many ways. Just as fiction writers
are on constant lookout for things that people say, which they then
store away for future use in their characters' dialogue, so we can all
be alert to all kinds of things that will be useful to our own creativity.
Daydreams and sleep dreams and the things we notice with all our
senses can all be food for thought and fire our imagination and
creative zest.

But ideas can also come to us through our sixth sense as we saw
in the last section, arriving spontaneously in our minds. As well as
practising inviting and noticing them in meditation, we can get better
and better at 'receiving' them simply by pausing now and then and
being ready to heed them.

You'll know the times you're most likely to be able to focus and
your 'sixth sense antennae' are at their most alert. It depends on our
personal body clock – some people are at their best, this way, early in
the morning; some at another time. Certainly, for me, when I wake
up in the morning is the time I'm likely to naturally be still, peaceful
and alert to inspirations and ideas coming to me. I know others who
most enjoy this awareness before they go to sleep at night, but this is
impossible for me as I'm pretty much asleep the minute I get into bed!
Or perhaps you are able to lie down for an 'inspiration oasis' in the
middle of the day...

There is something about lying down that works well. You are
more likely to hover on the brink of light sleep than you are when
meditating, and this particular state of relaxation encourages
creative inspiration just as much. Enjoy it – it feels good physically
to relax this way and it's a little bit of bliss when a fresh idea or new
perception arrives.

If you wish, it can also be a time of prayer for help with your
creativity – for inspiration and a sense of the right way forward.

Insight

Inspiration can come to us spontaneously in times of meditation,
contemplation, prayer and simply 'being in the moment' of our awareness.
Perhaps it arrives from our own subconscious, perhaps from another

dimension or energy we don't yet understand but so often feel is there – perhaps the creator of our world. I don't claim to understand it but I call it the 'sacred sense'. While science searches for the answers, we, as people born creative, can enjoy keeping an open mind. All we have to do to let our creativity flow this way is remember to be aware of inspiration and creative help as it comes to us.

Many of us sometimes experience a deep sense of longing without knowing exactly what the longing is for. I believe it is the longing for us to pay attention to two things – our creativity, and our connection with the sacred sense. When we do, our creativity and soul flourish and we feel at peace and fully alive.

6 POINTS OF REFLECTION

1 Imagination is such a fantastic resource for our creativity and it is there at your disposal whenever you want or need to use it. It's like giving your brain a holiday because it takes you out of yourself and lets you explore to your heart's content.

2 Don't fear boredom – use it as a foundation from which to spring into creativity.

3 Take time out to be idle now and then. In quiet, unproductive times we compost all kinds of experience, incubate new ideas and replenish energy levels.

4 Have you meditated today yet? If not, set aside a little time – a few minutes will do, though more would be especially good – to slip into the peace of it, recharge your batteries and perhaps tune into creative inspiration.

5 Take time, too, to feel a part of the extraordinary world we live in and all its wonder and complexity. You are here in this moment, this year, this millennium. Feel your presence and give thanks.

6 And take a moment as well to 'listen' to your creative needs and longings. When you pay them attention they will respond gladly.

10

·····

Process or product? The joy of creative process for its own sake – and how it unlocks your creativity

In this chapter you will learn:
* *how to engage in the creative process*
* *about the joy of an end product*
* *about the emotional release of being creatively productive*
* *about the healing power of being creative.*

Being and becoming, moment and meaning

It may be that you want to embrace your creativity in life generally and have no express plans to use it for work or in any way to make an end product. You simply wish to express your creativity by living more creatively in all kinds of ways and to enjoy the wonderful feeling of being 'in flow'.

Or perhaps your work or other interests involves creation of a product of some kind. It could be in any field – the arts, manufacturing and service industries, media or science – and you might be an employee, self-employed or working voluntarily for others or on a personal hobby or mission. But whatever it is, it's important to you that you come up with the goods and you want to use your creativity to the full to do so.

Both routes are absolutely understandable and have their own merit. But whereas it's fine to enjoy being creative without necessarily producing something, it would be a shame not to appreciate the results if there are some. And if we focus only on the product, we need to take care we don't miss out on the pleasure of the creative process. A balance is needed.

So, however goal-oriented you are, whether it's your nature or a demand of your job, you needn't get fixated on that alone and miss the joy of creative flow. Even if you've previously seen work as a means to a result and/or a financial income, with a cathartic shift of attitude you can begin to love the whole process. It needn't just be satisfying at the end – it can be fulfilling as you proceed. And there is a great bonus: the more you enjoy being creative, the more you expand your capacity to be so and it will flow and flourish to the full.

Likewise, if you already love being creative but have shied away from paying attention to what you produce and appreciating it – you have much enjoyment to explore.

Insight
When the process and produce of creativity go hand in hand to give you pleasure and excitement, they give a great feeling of satisfaction and fulfilment.

Of course, for someone whose creativity flows in their everyday life and through a particular interest or hobby, the product is very much less important than the process. For a professional, it's the other way round. Let's take a look at both.

The joy of creative process for its own sake – and how it unlocks your creativity

From original thoughts to making something new, from imaginative parenting to a sideways look at life, our creativity can light up just about every aspect of our lives. Creativity is central to us – always there, always available to give us zest and understanding, help us through, help us be our true original, unique self. The more we're aware of it, the more pleasure it gives us.

Creativity is such a fantastic gift and, as well as the intrinsic enjoyment of it, we can delight in sharing our appreciation and showing the joy of the creative path to others, too. Let's dispel the persistent myth that people should be self-effacing about their creativity and, unless they become celebrated in their field, keep quiet about it. If that is someone's true preference, so be it. But, if it's not, it's actually rather pretentious. So, if you really adore being creative, then for goodness' sake experience your pleasure to the full and don't be afraid to show it!

A new friend once told me about her first impression of me: 'I couldn't believe your obvious enthusiasm and enjoyment of your work,' she said. 'I'm friends with two highly creative people who are completely different. They are so serious about their work – everyone's a bit scared to even ask them about it and, if we do, we talk in hushed tones. You're the opposite – you obviously love it and love sharing your thoughts and inspiring others. It's really refreshing!'

Sadly, creativity is viewed by some so seriously that it becomes full of angst and even misery. Far too many painters, for example, are defeated by what they see as their constant struggle to produce the art they want to or to attract the acclaim they long for and they become depressed. Then their work becomes a trial to them, so much so they may give up completely. Some even give up on life because they come to see their creative path as one of hardship and even as a kind of self-torture.

If only they had chosen instead to love their work, each day, for its own sake, it could have benefited their work and lives. Too many creative people are oversensitive to the negative opinion of themselves, their peers or the public, and they tend to develop a love/hate relationship with their work, or even fall out of love with it completely and see it as a penance.

Our relationship with our creativity is much like a love affair and marriage. We can weather the transition from the entrancing initial in-love stage to an equally deep but enduring love only if we understand the process by which it changes and grows, and help it thrive in a new way. For, just like love, creativity is a living thing that develops and needs your love and care every step of the way. Given this, it will repay you generously, lighting up your life and energizing and entertaining you all your life through.

In being obsessed with product and opinion, we lose sight of a vital facet of creativity – the pleasure and sense of release and freedom we feel as we express it. Take a moment now to do the following exercise. Jot down any positive thoughts or impressions these phrases bring up. Let your first thoughts on each flow onto the paper and write just as much as you wish – whether that's a word or two or reams:

> **Try this**
> If I let myself love my work as I'm doing it, it would feel...
>
> I would...
>
>   (e.g. ...phone up X to tell them all about it.)
>
> I'd like to share my joy and inspiration with others by...
>
> I can encourage my creativity by...

Love your creativity with passion. Care for your creativity with tenderness. Ignite it with excitement. Soothe it with gentleness. Fight for it like a mother tiger. Your creativity is a part of you – a wonderful, life-transforming part. Be brave and true to your process and enjoy it.

Insight
> When we create, we express ourselves; we change, however subtly; we grow; we live and – if we wish – we feel the flow of love and joy that are inherent in the process if only we take care to pay attention, notice and accept it.

Engaging in the process

Most people would like to be creative but either believe they're not or that they haven't time. As we've seen, everyone is creative and, with recognition of this, a little nurturing of self-esteem and lots of help in getting going, our creativity can grow wings and learn to fly.

But wherever you are on the path – from just beginning to being an old timer – and whether you are an enthusiastic amateur or a professional, it can be difficult to start a creative process and to summon the dedication to see it through to the end.

Like most other practices, even the most pleasurable ones like being creative, the less we do it, the less likely we are to do it. However much we would like to, the effort of practising daunts us. We make promises to ourselves – tomorrow, next week, when I'm on vacation, next year when I'm not so busy – and suddenly years have rolled by without us doing what we long to do – to be creative.

We can all start to be creative. We can all resume being creative after a pause. We can all reverse a slide into not being creative. To get going all you need to do is...

- ▶ recognize your longing to be creative
- ▶ decide that, whatever it takes, you're going to be
- ▶ commit to a certain amount of practice (be positive but realistic – it's better to set aside half an hour once a week than an hour a day, if it means you're actually going to do it)
- ▶ take that first step – do something creative TODAY!

Ways to start the process

It's astonishing how we find ways to put off doing what we actually are longing to do. I love writing on a subject dear to my heart, but do I leap into action first thing inthe morning when I switch the computer on? Oh no... I find any manner of things to do before I can start. Actually, the excuses we can come up with are very creative in their own right: 'I've just got to answer a few emails / sort that file out' or 'I wonder if there are any bargains on eBay?' or 'Oh – I'll just visit such and such a website very quickly.'

And then I suddenly realize that, if I don't get started RIGHT NOW, there won't be a hope of getting my daily word count target done. So then – there's nothing else for it – I get going. And immediately my fingers hit the keys, my mind and creativity kick into action, energy flows, and I'm in my element. I keep going, with breaks along the way for a cup of coffee or tea, until I make target (for I'm one of those people who does need one), towards the end relishing the thought of the satisfaction of going past the winner's post and the reward of enjoying the late afternoon and evening.

Have you ever been swimming in the sea? Then you know the feeling. It's much like getting into icy-cold water – once you take the plunge and start swimming it feels fantastic, holds you up and makes your heart sing with gladness. If you're not a swimmer, think of an analogy that's apt for you – something you adore doing once you 'jump in' and get going. Whenever you're itching to do something creative but procrastinating for all you're worth, take your analogy in your hands and use it to spur you on.

Key factors in the creative process that are applicable to all of us are:

- ▶ the decision to start (for me helped by a target and/or deadline)
- ▶ the determination to keep going through the initial few minutes when it may feel clunky
- ▶ the pleasure of the process and getting in flow
- ▶ coffee/tea breaks – they're a good incentive and they replenish our energy and our resolve
- ▶ the lure of going past the finishing post
- ▶ the anticipation of relaxing afterwards in the glow of having been creative.

Your creative process may well vary hugely but all of the above are part of the creative process. Don't dismiss or underestimate the value of each one. Remember...

- ▶ Make that decision to do it and start.
- ▶ Like any exercise, as long as you persist you'll soon get your second wind.
- ▶ Give yourself permission and indeed insist that you consciously encourage yourself to enjoy the process; that way you'll avoid getting stressed or negative about it. Enjoy it! It's something you long to do and you're doing it – what could be better?
- ▶ Let yourself have that 'yes!' moment for staying the course. You deserve it – and the memory of it will help you every time you engage in the creative process again.
- ▶ When you're done, relish the feeling of having been creative and commit to enjoying the rest of the day fully.

Savouring every bit of the creative process this way belies the myth that creativity's innate nature demands a certain level of angst. It doesn't and it needn't. However, of course all sorts of emotions may feed our creativity and be caused by it, too, but we don't have to stress about them or let their energy drag us down. We can safely limit our emotional responses so they don't damage us.

Think, for example, of watching a film that moves you in some way. You are resonating with and responding to the story or the way the film has been directed and shot. But however emotional you are, it doesn't stress you out. It can be just the same for the film-maker. However much emotion they pour into the production and feel about it, they can choose not to get anxious about it. Just as medics and counsellors learn not to take their patients' emotions home with them, so can we learn to release our emotions in our creativity without letting their energy make us anxious. (In fact, it can dissolve anxiety and heal us generally – but more on this later in the chapter.)

When you and your creativity are flying together

The best part of the creative process is when we lose all self-consciousness and our work flows as though it's effortless, even though, depending on what we're doing, we may be putting in a lot of effort. But the energy is there for us as if we've been given wings and exactly the right weather conditions and airflows to support us and carry us along. Much has been written about this experience, but we don't need to analyse it. Let's just enjoy it when it happens. It's a kind of heaven. It's been called many things:

- ▶ being in flow / in the zone / in the moment / in the groove
- ▶ feeling the vibes
- ▶ flying
- ▶ being at one with the universe.

What would be your name for it? Have fun choosing or thinking up your own impression and name. Let it happen as much as possible in your life by doing your creative thing often, willingly and enthusiastically, and that way you'll create the right climate and conditions for it.

Flow or fly? It's the same thing and it feels just great.

More tips for enjoying the creative process

- ▶ Use **music** to get afloat – a-flow – aloft! I practised today letting my fingers 'dance' as they moved around the keys as I typed to a wonderful French song on the radio. The melody, the rhythm, even the sound of the words I didn't completely understand, swept me up and fed into the flow of the writing process. It helped me clarify the point I was working on and gave me an idea for a new, exciting segment.

- Keep your goal in mind if you like (as long as it doesn't daunt you) but remember to **celebrate small successes** along the way – an original thought, a new idea, something beautifully made and so on. It will hearten you and speed you on your way with love and a sense not just of accomplishment but that you are accomplishing something.
- **Stretch yourself.** Lengthen your stride or do something you wouldn't normally. Be brave. Experiment. Stretching loosens our creative muscles and lets energy flow.
- **Smudge the outlines.** Let yourself go out of control now and then, overstepping boundaries, letting the colours, words, etc., flow where they want. Like a painting, your creativity wants to live and discover itself, explore the possibilities and discover new potential.
- **Kick out your inner negative critic.** By all means step back, review, adjust, be constructive. But refuse to cripple yourself with negativity. Positivity will enable you and give you wings.
- **Pace yourself.** Let your creativity take however long it takes. Live with it. Love it. Run alongside it. Support it with all your heart, mind, body and soul.

Now try this 'get going' exercise:

Try this
Write for as long as you wish on this subject:

'What I really want to say is...'

I decided to try it myself as a 'get going' inspiration just now when I wasn't sure what I was going to write next. I had no idea what I would write but the words flowed out of me. They were, totally unexpectedly, the introduction to this book rather than part of this chapter.

Often we don't quite know where our creativity is going or wants to go until we let it take form through the medium best known to us – words. When you let it come through this way, you will find yourself tapping into whatever it is you are itching or deep down aching to say and/or do.

The exercise above is sister to the exercise in the following section. You could do them together or apart. You may find they are interchangeable. Either way, let them be a trigger for you whenever you are feeling a bit unsure or blocked. Enjoy.

The joy of an end product

Try this
As above, write as much as you wish on this subject:

'What I would really like to create is...'

followed by:

'I would like to approach this goal by...'

Together these are a particularly good starting point when you want to produce something and are searching for direction. At art school, these statements and the train of thought that followed led us into and then through virtually each project we did. Often we would be bewildered by the module's title and requirement, and this exercise infallibly helped us find our way not just into and through the brief but right to a fulfilling conclusion to it.

Is it important to produce something? No, not always. As we've seen, often process is all. But often, too, and always for some, we *do* want or need to have a product of our work to call our own. For those professionals whose creative talent and expertise are crucial to their work, it is not just important but essential.

In conversation with professional creative people in many diverse fields, I was struck over and over again by their passion for what they produced:

▶ 'The excitement of product is dynamic. One person's success impacts on all of us in the team, producing a new wave of creative ideas, focus and energy,' said an employee of an engineering company.
▶ 'In business,' said an entrepreneur, 'producing a result creatively and well is the best – it's incredibly satisfying!'

- ▶ 'When I'm pleased with a painting,' said an artist, 'it's like a special kind of joy singing in my heart.'
- ▶ A carer said: 'Knowing you've improved the quality of someone's life is all.'

Even when producing an end result is not integral to your work or purpose, it's not only totally permissible but very desirable that you enjoy the fruits of any creative process. Your creativity is a part of you, so what you come up with is very much your offspring. In some way, even if its value lies in only what you've learned through its production, the end result is worth keeping and it may at some stage prove useful or even precious to you.

I used to bin or destroy material I'd written and paintings and drawings that didn't – whether in truth or just in my opinion – come up to scratch. But when I went to art college we were taught to keep everything.

Insight

Just because you don't want to display your work or you think it wouldn't sell, it doesn't necessarily mean it has no merit. In any case, it's always interesting to be able to look back and trace your creative development.

While it's fine for work we're not sure of or simply not mad about to be stored out of sight, I'm a great advocate of keeping anything we really like on show. The same friend who was surprised by my open enjoyment and enthusiasm in being creative also told me later that the first time she visited my house she had been inspired by seeing several of my paintings on the walls including one where the oil paint was still wet. 'I would never have had the confidence to display any of my work at all, let alone immediately,' she said, 'but seeing you do it with such pleasure made me realize it's fine to.'

I won't tell you it doesn't matter what other people think because to some extent it does. We can learn a lot from others' thoughtful observations, and their spontaneous impressions and interest, as long as this isn't accompanied by negative criticism, can be very rewarding and uplifting. It's also a tremendous boost when an employer, entrepreneur or purchaser approves of your work.

However, it's central to our creativity that all of us, including the professionals among us, remember that far and away the most important things are:

▶ our own willingness to participate in the magical charisma of our individual creative process
▶ our engagement in and appreciation of the catharsis creativity offers
▶ our personal satisfaction in a job well done
▶ our own pleasure in the product.

The emotional release of being creatively productive

Being creatively productive also offers a feel-good way to express emotion both therapeutically and constructively.

Everyday life offers countless opportunities. For instance, just this morning a friend emailed to share his strong opinions about an article that had appeared in the review section of a broadsheet newspaper. He took issue with several of the writer's points and also with remarks of two of the people he quoted. I agreed with him and urged him to write to the paper in response. A little later he emailed me again, attaching a copy of the letter he'd written, and was clearly delighted he'd written it. The letter was well thought out and expressed and was lit up by his evident passion for and knowledge of the subject.

So often when we are riled by something, we seethe for a while and then let it go without really resolving it. How much better it is to address the exasperation or other troubling emotion, by harnessing your creative energy and putting it to good use. Expression feels good in itself, but when it has a product it's immensely satisfying. In this case, my friend enjoyed writing his letter, felt pleased afterwards and stood to do some constructive good, too, and set several wrongs right.

Insight
In harnessing creative thoughts and ideas and directing them into the production of something that others can share, we release the energy of our emotions and gain a hugely rewarding sense of usefulness, satisfaction and fulfilment.

The healing power of being creative

In fact, there's a sense of release – of sheer liberation – whenever our creativity flows. If ever you feel out of sorts for no apparent good reason, it's probably because you need to be creative. No good pretending that, if you ignore this longing, it will go away. It won't. It will keep badgering you no matter how many barriers you erect and no matter how many padlocks you put on it. It will tap away at your happiness and, if you don't recognize it, you'll continue to feel intermittently or perhaps constantly frustrated.

If I'm squashing my creative drive, I'm likely to feel irritable despite my normal easygoing temperament. It took me many years to realize that the cause of this irritation and discomfort is almost always a frustrated need to unlock my creativity. Nowadays, as soon as I register I'm feeling grouchy, I ask the question: 'What shall I do that's creative?' Then either I make a start or, if that's not possible, I set aside some time for it later in the day.

Creativity is the best tonic in the world. The minute you start doing something creative, or even promise yourself that you soon will, you feel better. Irritation dissolves along with any physical manifestation of the tension that accompanies it. Attending to our creative needs is as refreshing as showering or swimming. Tension is swooshed away and energy and feel-good hormones flow again.

Insight
Happiness, activities we enjoy and freedom from stress are key ingredients of good health – and creativity dispenses them all abundantly.

If this is true in 'normal' times when we are well and happy, it is just as true in the bad times, too.

Creativity can be a healing friend when our lives are in the doldrums. When I've ached with sadness in bereavement, writing has been like a crutch, keeping me going, bandaging the pain and, in time, allowing me to see glimmers of light with the promise that life will be good again.

Belle, an artist, told me that, though she was broken-hearted when her relationship broke up, she found herself recovering almost palpably when she poured her sorrow and outrage into paint as she worked on a series of huge canvases. Similarly, Antony, an office worker, said that he only started to get over the shock of being made redundant when he started to think *creatively* about new ways forward: 'The minute I started exploring not just possible openings in a similar field but all kinds of other options, I began to feel better. I did find another office job eventually, but knowing there were other possibilities was inspiring and altered my whole demeanour and outlook.'

Insight

As well as helping us heal by safely allowing us to live through and discharge the emotions and trauma of sorrow, loss and change, our creativity helps us move on, recharging our energy and positivity. And, in resonating with it, others may be helped, too.

Being and becoming, moment and meaning (again)

'Everyone keeps talking about the meaning of art and creativity,' a man said in a debate recently, 'and we are all artists in our own way – perhaps, for instance, in parenting skills or the way we love or work. I think that's true. Definitely, we can all be creative. It might be in an original thought, or a personal way of doing something in the art, craft, design and manufacturing fields, or in any aspect of life – but when we are creative we feel at home with ourselves.

In such moments – whether it's literally a moment or several hours – the meaning of *your* life becomes clear. And you are at one with it. It might happen when you are putting huge, painstaking effort into something. Or it might be there in a spontaneous, unworked-for flash of insight or inspiration. But either way, deep in your soul and – *with* your soul – you rejoice.

However, the same man in the debate went on to make a typical cynical comment: 'But of course there's nothing new. Everything has been said and done before. Who do we think we are to think we can contribute something original?' But that's the astonishing joy of it. It hasn't all been done and said before, let alone thought. No one thinks the same way as you. You are unique and have the ability to think and therefore be creative differently from anyone else on this planet.

Yes, we love to retrace the steps of the thinkers and artists who have trodden this path before us and there's nothing wrong with that. But even when you are exploring old concepts and arguments, you can bring your personal style and slant to it.

So think! Never stop thinking, never stop feeling and never, ever, stop being curious.

Keep asking and, to the best of your ability, keep answering or searching for the answers to the questions.

That way your creativity leaps for joy and soars and so will you.

Insight

High-five it rapturously when you have a thought that is original to you. Your brain and creativity love recognition and approval, and the more you give it to them the better they will serve you.

6 POINTS OF REFLECTION

1 So often we are fixated on what we're making or working towards. Instead, think in terms of enjoying the process and the flow of your creativity.

2 As you work or progress in any aspect of your life, live in the moment and concentrate on what you're doing right now. Pay attention to what's going on around you, too, and how other people are. Be mindful of all that's going on.

3 Of course, the product of what you're doing or the end result may be very important to you and that's fine. Nonetheless, see it as part of the whole process and not as the be-all and end-all.

4 Reflect on the emotions of the day and how you felt during times of creativity and when you finished doing something. Being in touch with these feelings will increase your awareness of your creativity and enable you to enjoy them all the more in future.

5 Next time you are specifically being creative or just thinking and living life creatively, sense how healing it feels and be aware of how it benefits your physical and emotional health.

6 Every moment you are on the path of your life. It's a creative path and you are a creative, wonderful human being. Take joy in the moment as you pause on the path.

11

A lifestyle that nurtures your creativity

In this chapter you will learn about:
- *how your home can also be home to your creativity*
- *how you can use your leisure time creatively*
- *the potentially inspiring interplay between you, others and your creativity*
- *everyday creative choices.*

Your home is also home to your creativity

We spend around a third of our lives at home so it's bound to have a substantial influence on our wellbeing and, it follows, on our creativity. Added to the fundamental wholesome feeling of being safe and comfortable is the massive inspiration that we get from having a home that pleases us visually and in other ways, too.

With a little attention to our individual taste, it's easy to choose colours and other things we like. We can use paint, fabric and pictures, for example, to create a look that pleases us. That way, whenever we look around us while we're in our homes – at any time from waking until we go to sleep at the end of the day – we have the gift of a visually delightful experience. You don't necessarily need beautiful things – much-loved objects can give us just as much and sometimes even more pleasure – and it's absolutely not necessary to spend much. Creative thinking and finding bargains are pleasurable in themselves and can give the personalized style you want.

Our homes say a lot about our self-esteem. Appreciating and maximizing the happiness that your home gives you is an expression not just of your self-respect but also self-love. And oh, we do need to love ourselves! When we do, generously and warmly, we're emotionally equipped to be able to love others as generously and to appreciate their love for us. The circle goes round and round and feels great, and is a foundation for us to appreciate our creativity and the creative choices we make.

Insight
Wherever you live, look for the love and any other beauty you can find and let it inspire you. Let it uplift you in the moment. It may light up your whole life.

In fact, the essence of a home is love. And wherever we live, even in the direst of circumstances, we can fill it with love. I've just read a true story about a young Jewish boy who was interned in a concentration camp in the Second World War. Like all the prisoners, he was treated like dirt by the guards and he assumed he must actually be worthless. Then one day he decided to think about the situation rationally and he made a list of the good things about himself. He was, he realized, kind, honest and hardworking. Above all, he was loving and lovable. He survived and when he grew up he spent the rest of his life in a career helping others. His creative thinking and willingness to love himself lifted him out of the horror and helped him forge a blessed life full of love.

CASE STUDY

Here's another example of the way we can find inspiration and hope in any circumstances. I remember meeting the artist and doctor Kenneth McCall and seeing the series of ink pictures he drew in an internment camp in the Far East in the same war. He was provided with ink and a brush to make a graphic record of the day-to-day life in the camp. The only paper he could get was toilet paper. Each drawing was a monochrome scene. Factual. Stark. When I came to the last one, tears flowed down my face. It was in a vibrant colour that he'd somehow procured and showed the glorious hue and beauty of the morning glory climbing the compound fence. He told me later that the joy of the flowers against the sombre grey of the camp helped him and his wife hold on to hope and help the other prisoners do so as well. He, too, spent the rest of his life helping others, as did his wife. He gave me a painting of his of a girl dancing in a wood and, whenever I look at it, I smile with the joy that shines through it. The couple's home was the prettiest house I have ever seen. Inside it was homely and utterly charming. Their love for themselves, each other, their family and any guest shone through, along with their gift for healing and their abundant creativity.

> Try this
> Make some notes about your home and its potential:
>
> ▶ What do you like about it?
> ▶ How do you feel when you get home?
> ▶ What could you do to make it an even better place to be?
> ▶ What is an easy first step towards doing that?
> ▶ What else can I do or make for my home that expresses my creativity?
> ▶ If I were going to buy my home a present, what would it be?
>
> Above all, remember to pay attention to your home and fill it with love.

How you can use your leisure time creatively

Our free time is potentially our greatest creative resource. All we have to do is see it as such and decide what we want to do with it. But work and the various pressures of life are tiring, and it's all too easy to 'crash out' when we have time off and either do nothing or fritter it away on aimless stuff that leaves us unsatisfied. We probably complain that 'we don't have time' to be creative – but in our hearts we know we do have time, and just wish we could gear ourselves up to take full advantage of it. But before we know it, the next workday comes around and, instead of feeling energized and up for it, we're more likely to feel reluctant or decidedly unwilling.

Sometimes, of course, it's good and very necessary to have a complete rest doing nothing and catching up on sleep. As you rest, your mind and creativity will be free to contemplate, consciously or subconsciously, what they'd like you to do next. When you feel refreshed and ready to do something, you might have no particular project, plan or purpose in mind and simply want to have fun exploring something creative. In that case, I highly recommend a technique my sister Penny and I developed one day when we were having a go at marbling. We got that completely wrong but in the process of trying we discovered by chance a fabulous way of having brilliant creative fun and letting our imaginations run riot. Since then we've introduced several people to it and it's fascinating to see how, although we're using the same paints and process, we come up with completely different pictures. We call it 'splodging' and I hope you will have as much fun with it as we do.

Try this: The creative touchstone of 'splodging'

1 In a flat-bottomed sink, a large tray with a rim or a baking/ roasting tin, pour a little water – about half a centimetre deep.

2 Using acrylic paints, choose some colours that appeal to you and which you think will look good together. We like to use five or six, but others have preferred just using two or three or even a single colour.

3 Onto a palette – ice-cube trays or the foil containers from a box of chocolates make excellent 'impromptu' palettes – squeeze several 'splodges' of paint, each about an inch deep. If you're using a flat palette, be careful to keep the colours separate. Add a little water to each one and mix well – so that the paint is soft but not completely fluid.

4 Now use a teaspoon or a small palette knife to drop some of each colour into your water bath. You can leave the little piles of paint you make as they are or, if you like, you can move them around a little to make shapes or patterns. I sometimes move the palette around a little bit so that the colours swirl out into the water.

5 Now take a piece of card – we use A5 or A4 size and a weight of 300 gsm – put it down flat on top of the water-and-paint bath and press very gently so that it makes contact with the paint. Immediately lift it out. You can now either hold it flat to keep the design, or tilt it to let the colours flow in other directions.

6 Put it somewhere flat to dry. Every few minutes lift it to prevent it sticking to the surface beneath. The card does buckle up a bit but, once dry, it can be flattened under a heavy book.

7 Consider making a print from your artwork by placing it, while still wet, face down on another piece of card. Quite often we get the best effects from such prints.

8 Use the paint bath over and over with new pieces of card, adding more paint if you wish.

Now comes the miracle. Usually we can't stop looking at the instant paintings we've made and often we find ourselves suddenly seeing pictures in them and all we have to do is draw or paint them in to define them. It's extraordinary the way this process frees your creativity. You might suddenly see an animal, for instance, or a landscape, and choose to develop that image, or simply use the abstract as a background for another design. I recently was about to write off one of my splodge paintings but, just before it got filed away, I suddenly saw that one corner of it was a beautiful snow scene in a forest and, with a little bit of help from some computer software, I had created the design for my next Christmas card.

You can also embellish your splodge paintings with any of the following:

▶ gold or silver paint (sprays can give a magical effect)
▶ glitter
▶ varnish – just little bits painted in will catch the light and the eye...

or use digital imaging software to play with the colours and the design to your heart's content.

As well as the fun you get out of splodging, the creativity it inspires flows on in other areas of life. One friend who hadn't painted for years has now taken it up again with passion and excitement. Two young people we splodged with were so energized when they left that they talked all the way home about different business ideas they'd had on the back boiler for months, decided on one and then went on to develop it into a fully fledged commercial plan.

As the paintings come out of the water-and-paint bath they are so gloriously inchoate that they seem to be bursting with new life, just waiting for you to give them a helping hand to become what they want to become. And the special bonus is that, no matter what the creative area you usually work in, splodging liberates your imagination across the board.

Other suggestions to let your creativity flow

▶ Design something new – it could be something as simple as working out a new layout for your vegetable allotment.
▶ Write a poem.

- ▶ Sing your heart out – your voice, your style, your way.
- ▶ Explore. Get a map and go for a walk somewhere you've never walked before.
- ▶ Make something – a cake, a bookcase, a jumper, anything... Make it as original and whacky as you like – a pure, unbridled expression of you.
- ▶ Think about what book you would really like to read. If it's a novel, reflect on the kind of story, characters, emotions and style that most appeal to you. How would you write it yourself? Or if it's a non-fiction book – can you spot a glaring hole in the market? You don't actually have to write it – this is about having fun thinking about it and letting your imagination and passion flow.

The potentially inspiring interplay between you, others and your creativity

Everyone we meet can be an inspiration, as there is always an exchange of energy and we can 'catch' this energy, even if it's negative, and create something from it – a thought, an idea, an emotion – anything that strikes us.

My mother, a wonderful nurse, loved people and she was fascinated by them. Often when we were out somewhere together I'd say: 'Mum, come back – where are you?' And she'd tell me, in hushed, rapt excitement, about some perception she'd made into the life of whomever had caught her eye – it was always well observed and intuitive. It uplifted her as did her love of any film, novel or autobiography that took her into the lives and minds of other people. And she used the intuition and inspiration extremely creatively in the way she empathized with the patients she cared for so well. Thus, creativity and inspiration expanded and intensified her gift for healing and understanding others.

My sister and I have both inherited her love of 'standing in others' shoes' as a way to be better able to encourage their own inspiration and/or route to healing. And, like my mother, I especially love books and films where you almost feel you are the lead character. It flows into my creativity, especially when I'm writing or painting, and also as a counsellor, in person or as an agony aunt, through the inspiration of understanding and choosing a holistic path to finding solutions, resolutions and healing. Like Naomi Ozaniec, the author of another Teach Yourself title, *Beat Stress with Meditation*, I go back to C. S. Lewis's *Chronicles of Narnia* regularly. Through his characters flows his wisdom, compassion and the deep sense of 'something beyond' that have helped and encouraged me throughout my life and which I try to pass on to others in my work and play.

> Try this
> How does your interaction with others inspire you? Over the next few days and weeks pay attention to the flow of energy you sense whenever you meet someone, and think how it can feed into your imagination, inspiration and your creative flow.

Others' energy levels have a big effect on all of us. You might unconsciously be influenced by another's hidden depression or tension and wonder why you feel vaguely out of sorts or irritable around them. We are more likely to consciously register it when the company of someone upbeat lifts our spirits. We talk of being energized by someone – and that is exactly what happens. Their energy and zest for life resonates with ours. It's uplifting, healing and inspirational.

> Try this
> Reflect for a few moments on times when another's company has depressed your mood or spirits. Did you recognize what was happening at the time, or only afterwards notice your deflation. And did you realize you were picking up on their depression or other negative emotion? Then think of those whose presence uplifts and inspires you.

The more creative we become, the more sensitive we are likely to become to others' emotions and how their emotions interact with our own. Obviously, we can't rule out from our lives all those who have a generally negative effect on us, and it's especially important to give them our time and support generously if they are ill or have problems. But, because it has such a detrimental effect on our own spirits and creativity, it's imperative that we don't overdo the time we spend with them. You can also limit the effect, to some extent, by imagining an 'energy barrier' around you that will protect you from negative influence. It really does work.

Insight

As much as possible, choose to keep company with people who energize you in a good way, uplifting you and leaving you feeling the better from your interaction with them. And do your best to do the same for others – consciously lifting your energy so that it sparkles with theirs and makes them feel good. Then their creativity and yours will be elevated by at least a notch or two – maybe several!

The effect your love of life has on your creativity

Loving life is a creative catalyst. It's powerful – more powerful than we can probably ever realize. It heightens the bar of our creative energy as the feel-good hormones it releases lift us physically and mentally. It's better than any drug we can smoke or swallow or inject because it's natural and totally beneficial to our health and wellbeing.

Encourage love and creative energy to flow through you by tuning into the wonder of people, animals, art, science and all kinds of other elements of this amazing world. However it all came into being, developed and continues to flourish, the earth is an astonishing miracle of complex creation – way, way beyond the scope of our present understanding.

Insight

Just think: your creativity is a part of our world and universe and whatever other dimensions lie beyond or somehow parallel to it.

Your creativity is part of it. It's energy is yours.

Be inspired. Feel it. Tingle with joy.

Creative oases

We've talked before of places where inspiration seems to surround and flow through us:

▶ Be aware of yours and visit them often.
▶ Carry a notebook with you – it's so easy to be convinced you'll remember ideas and visions that come to you, but in reality you probably won't.

- ▶ Be still and silent.
- ▶ Feel the peace and, perhaps, a sense of anticipation and excitement, too.
- ▶ Tune in: be aware with all your antennae.
- ▶ Praise something. Anything good in your life. The love you feel in this special place. Your presence in this place and this world. Give thanks.

Insight

We can find special places wherever we travel – and on holiday the sense of being at rest is particularly conducive to recognizing and tuning into them. But actually they are there just as much in our normal everyday life and surroundings – it's just a case of being alert to them. You might, for instance, have a chair you like to sit in where your creativity always seems especially vibrant, a walk you love where thoughts come to you easily, or a local ancient building whose spirit or energy resonates with yours.

Using your senses to enhance your creativity

Creativity is a great friend of our senses and loves to accompany them. It's there whenever one of our senses lifts us out of ourselves. Creativity is there...

- ▶ ...when we're revelling in the **scent** of something. Think of the bliss of the fragrance of your favourite flowers and how a rush of pleasure flows through you, washing you with creative inspiration, too. Another favourite scent of mine is the smell of a horse's coat: I press my face into it and drink deep and am overcome with the love for this gracious creature that smells sooo good! What are your favourite scents that lift you into another plane?
- ▶ ...when we're **tasting** something that overwhelms us with its deliciousness. I've way too many favourites to list here. Have fun making your list. Some remembered tastes take us back to a special time, flooding us with such nostalgia we're spurred to make something creative from it. Others take us forward creatively as, again, we find ourselves wanting to share the feeling.
- ▶ ...when we **listen** intently to music, voices, song, the wind – to so many unbelievably inspiring sounds. Think of sounds that move you and make a list.

▶ ...when we **listen mystically** for the sacred sense. Write or paint or dance or express your response in any way you like. What does it mean to you and how does it feel?

▶ ...when we **touch** anything we love – anything whose surface, texture, form intrigues us. Let the sensation flow through your body. Wonder at the diversity of texture. For example, the incredibly spiky feel of a thistle flower and the total contrast of thistledown – so soft in its unique way. We tend to underestimate the power of touch. Like music, it can be healing. When you stroke a purring cat, the sense of touch and sound resonate with your body's healing system. What are your favourite things to touch?

▶ ...when we **see** the humanity and other wonderful aspects of the world all around us; when we see the beauty of art we love. What delights you visually?

▶ when we experience the senses of **sexual attraction** and **desire**. We don't need to be romantically or sexually involved with anyone to notice and appreciate the excitement and pleasure of our feminine or masculine sensuality. Appreciation has always stirred our inspiration and is an ongoing source of all kinds of art, craft and various other creative endeavours. Think of the feeling of being in love and relive it in your mind. Enjoy it to the full and notice the feeling of being in flow and how this dances hand in hand with the in-flow experience of being creative.

▶ ...when we feeling the **emotions** that our appreciation of our senses raise in us and other feelings that come and go throughout each day. How have your emotions affected you today? How did or could you express them creatively?

▶ ...when we feel the **flow of creativity** as it brushes alongside us and, if we let it, it lifts us up and carries us along with it in an ecstasy of completeness and surety. Think of the last time this happened to you. Introduce it into your life as an everyday happening with any of the ideas and exercises in this book.

Insight
Being aware of your senses and the way that, in resonating with them, you are also in touch and harmony with your creativity is delectably inspiring. Your senses are a gift and at your disposal to appreciate every day in conjunction with your creativity.

The importance of noticing beauty and uniqueness

Our world is so full of beautiful and fascinating things it's like living among a smorgasbord of aesthetic and/or curious splendours. The natural world is, of course, teeming with visual and other delights, and while incomparable in diversity and quality, human design, craft, art and other enterprise are amazing, too, and have greatly added to the beauty around us. However, because we keep ourselves so occupied with the minutiae of life, and because we are so used to this constant visual kaleidoscope, we usually pay attention to only a fraction of it.

It's breathtaking to realize the extraordinary scope of the inspiration available to us simply by paying attention. Just take light, for instance. I look around me as I write and immediately see something I haven't noticed before: the way the sunlight is playing with the shadows on the ground and fence outside the window. The effect is so subtle and beautiful it blows me away. And I'm also fascinated by the way it is casting reflections on the window itself and illuminating the tiny particles of dust on the surfaces of the double glazing and highlighting the space between the panes – something you wouldn't normally see unless you looked very closely.

Try this

1 Look around you and take in any aspect of the minutiae around you or focus on one or two areas of what you can see.
2 Really look.
3 Seek out something fascinating or beautiful in it.
4 Feel the wonder and perhaps a little humility that you had never noticed this before or at least not paid much attention to it.
5 Ask yourself some questions about it: What thoughts, ideas, emotions does it stir in you? How was it made? What is its significance?
6 Reflect that, if such a tiny aspect of your surroundings had gone unnoticed, how many countless billions of unobserved wonders there are in the world beyond.
7 Think of the inspiration you have yet to tap – an inexhaustible source.

8   As you resonate with the beauty and creativity all around you
    in both natural and man-made things, reflect that you are both
    part of creation *and* a creative being. Treasure this gift and
    responsibility and feel – *always* feel – the energy and flow of
    universal creativity flowing through you, giving you the energy
    and ability you need, every day and every moment.

Everyday creative choices

Every day is full of opportunities to make good choices. Every day we
can aim to be:

▶ imaginative
▶ ingenious
▶ thoughtful
▶ kind
▶ helpful
▶ full of hope/optimism
▶ practical and constructive.

And every day you should stretch your creativity and keep it healthy
by asking questions and having thoughts like:

▶ 'What if...?'
▶ 'Let's imagine...'
▶ 'I wonder what would happen if...'
▶ 'Do you think...?'
▶ 'It's so interesting that...'
▶ 'It could be interesting if we...'
▶ 'I'm curious about...'
▶ 'Isn't it fascinating that...?'
▶ 'Perhaps there's another way...?'

We don't get everyday life right all the time – being positive, creative,
kind, and so on. But we can notice when we don't get it right and
resolve to try harder, do better. Living creatively, we keep thinking
of and working out ways to honour life – our own and others'. Every
day is potentially a work of art. It might be the simplest but still
incredibly beautiful thing, like filling a room you enter with light –
the light of love and happiness – or saying something complimentary

instead of being cutting, or smiling at someone you wouldn't normally acknowledge, or inspiring somebody in some way.

> 'I always believe in the good and that we are here to be good. You have to keep fighting (for idealism) and questioning.'
> **Cerys Matthews**

This isn't about being a goody two-shoes or Pollyanna-ish. It's about sensing the wonder of the greater picture and the love and goodness that flows in life and all around and through us.

Insight

Yes, of course there are tragedies and traumas in the world and, in people, evil, too. But we don't have to let that drag us down and make us feel there is no hope. There is always hope for an increasingly compassionate and mutually responsible worldwide civilization. And each one of us, in believing in the good and using our creative abilities in trying our best to be a part of it, can add to this essential good.

Just think, if more and more of us aim to light up life like this, what an amazing impact it will have. Don't be weighed down with what you can't do. Think instead of what you *can*! You are buzzing with the energy of creativity. Create goodness. Every day.

6 POINTS OF REFLECTION

1 Home is where the heart of your creativity is. Use your creativity to make it a continuously comfortable and inspiring place to be, and revel in it.

2 Remember not to fritter away your leisure time with unfulfilling bits and pieces. Of course, it's good to 'veg out' occasionally, but creativity loves an enquiring, vibrant mind. Connect with it and have fun together.

3 It's good to try something different once in a while to activate our creativity and give us new ideas.

4 So much of our enjoyment of life is about attitude. It's the same with our creativity. Think positively on both fronts as much as possible. It really is a choice we can make and it feels good.

5 Find or create a creative oasis or two where you know you can retreat when life's got you down or you feel you need to reconnect with the creative energy of the world. It could be in the country or a city – all that matters is that it's somewhere you feel at peace and safe from harm.

6 Our creativity loves it when we are alert to the beauty of the world, the love in it, its idiosyncrasies and wonders, be they small or large. You will love it, too. Awareness lights up our lives.

12

The whole spectrum of being creative

In this chapter you will learn:
- *how being creative gives you fulfilment*
- *about the life-enhancing habit of being creative*
- *how in being creative you reach out to others and touch them with your verve and happiness*
- *about the joy of being your true creative self*
- *about the synchronicity of creativity.*

The fulfilment of living creatively

There are as many benefits of being creative as there are ways to be creative. And that's an awful lot. Many of the things we do we choose to do and we can use our minds to make those choices. And with every single thing we do, we can choose what *attitude* we'll take when we do it as well as the *way* we do it.

It's only if we go through life on automatic pilot with our senses dulled down, or if we deny or belittle our creativity, that we push it under. By living mindfully, we stay alert to our wide-ranging capacity to be creative and all the myriad opportunities we have.

Some aspects of life are more obviously recognizable as being creative – our work and the way we work, the art, craft and other things we make, the way we use our imagination and ingenuity, the way we conduct our relationships with others, the way we love and connect with and use our other emotions, too.

So many ways. So much rich opportunity.

And the wonderful thing is that the more we put into being creative and living creatively, the more fulfilled we feel. It's as though we create an aura around us that is always with us, there for us, supportive, uplifting.

So practise. Practise engaging with your creativity every step of the way through life. It's such a friend, such an energy and source of energy, such an incredible blessing. Write your daily free-flow pages whatever happens. Think of something creative to do at least every day. Play creatively. Use your brain. Engage with others – *really* engage – and think, think, think about the way you are and they are, and about how you interact and how you might better interact.

It's about being mindful. When we are mindful, we are automatically creative because we're switched on to the moment. This moment now. Every moment we live. When you are present and aware of what's going on in and around you, you feel truly alive, connecting with the world around you and having your own ideas and thoughts and being interested in others' ideas and thoughts, too.

Feeling connected, love comes easily – flowing to us and from us and all around us. Creativity is part of love and life and the three, together, give us the most joyous sense of fulfilment – a taste of heaven on earth.

The habit of being intuitively creative

An idea comes into your mind and you know you want to produce it – to let it become and be. It could be through your painting or writing, music, work – any form of creativity. Perhaps it comes into your mind as a vision. Perhaps it comes out of the paint, or words or notes, or a business plan or whatever ingredients or things you are working with.

You give yourself up to it. Even if it is not like anything you've learned or seen or been taught, you allow it and enable it to come into being. It can be daunting if you have the germ of an idea but no clear vision of what the finished outcome will be. But you have to go with it in the hope that it will please you and others. It's exhilarating and utterly compelling. It gives you a thrill of intensity like nothing else.

Sometimes you need to work and work at it. Sometimes it flows so fast that it's there, happening as though in an instant. It flows as though of its own accord, and often it feels as though it is guiding you rather than the other way around.

The sooner you open yourself up to this and let it happen, the more it will and the easier it feels.

Never, ever feel that you don't have it in you to create something good. You do. Perhaps it's something you like, quietly and gently, to keep low key and to yourself. Perhaps it's something that will amaze others. It's very individual and all each of us can do is what we can, letting it happen by listening to the music of our creativity and our soul and by providing as best we can the right muse to help us feel the flow.

If you want to be creative, encourage yourself to have thoughts and ideas and to use your imagination and ingenuity, your abilities and emotions. And notice them, encourage and listen to them, let them flow and dance with you. In this book you've learned a lot of ways you can open up the creative arterial 'trunk roads'. Choose one or two each day and practise being creative. All it takes is the desire to be creative, the decision to practise and a 'Yes, I'm going to give it a go' attitude.

Poems don't get written if we don't let the words come into our minds and onto the paper.

No picture would get painted if we didn't dip the brush into the paint and make a mark.

Creativity happens when you do something *your* way.

And whether it's an original thought you simply register, or an idea that becomes something that changes the world, it feels good.

....

Insight
You don't have to wait years to have a creative moment. The more you encourage yourself to be creative on a daily basis and the more you live creatively in the moment, the more aware of your innate creative flow and zest you will be. It's always there for you, ready and willing.

....

The surprise, blessing and fun of creative awareness and the inspiration of ongoing learning

A good way to understand how creativity can light up our lives is to think of the excitement and sense of wonder that children have. They have so many new experiences, every day – so many things to see, taste, smell, hear and touch. They are naturally imaginative, too. The world is a wonderful playground and a mine of fascinating things to learn about.

We can be like that all our lives if we let ourselves – full of wonder and appreciation for the gift of life. Like a child:

▶ notice the beauty, the emotions, the extraordinary variety of life all around you
▶ let your natural creativity come through
▶ show your wonder at the magic of life and share it with others
▶ when no one is looking (or even when they are!) jump and/or dance for joy – feel your childlike exuberance – it's still there inside you!
▶ chuckle often – you know that wonderful way laughter bubbles up out of children? Sense that wonderful feeling inside yourself and let it out. We're not talking about snide humour or sarcasm here – the sheer joy of natural laughter comes from the delight we take in the world.

Insight
Fresh and spontaneous childlike awareness and appreciation are a huge help in unlocking our creativity and enjoying it. Another vital part of the key is to continue learning throughout our lives. When we are interested in life we tend to be interesting, and our creativity thrives, too.

I'm often shocked to hear someone write off an entire creative genre from their life. They'll claim, for instance, that they're not interested in art or music, but when you enquire further they'll say: 'I don't understand art,' or 'I never listen to music.' It's a bit like saying you don't like a certain food when you have never tasted it or have tasted it only badly cooked or prepared.

We can encourage our own creativity by increasing our appreciation of others'. When you recognize the reason you 'don't like something' is perhaps because you know little about it, try engaging your curiosity and, with an enthusiastically enquiring mind, expand your understanding. You'll expand your own creativity at the same time.

Try this
Choose something to consider that you wouldn't normally have taken any notice of, or felt you wouldn't like because of its genre. Take time to look at or otherwise consider it. You can do this with many things but looking at a painting is a particularly good way to practise the art of 'getting into something'. In the gallery, stand in front of a picture and ask yourself:

▶ Why do you feel you were drawn to it?
▶ What do you like about it?
▶ What don't you like about it?
▶ How has the artist used colour, shades and tones?
▶ How detailed is it and what do like about that in particular?
▶ Are there any nuances of the painting that interest you?
▶ How do you think the artist was feeling as they painted it?
▶ Why do others like it?
▶ How much do *you* like it?

When you get home, do some research on the artist and find out what you can about the painting, too:

▶ Do you like their other work?
▶ In the context of the art world and the period, how do/did they fit in?
▶ If you are a painter or would like to be, is this the kind of painting you would like to do?

That may be enough for your first consideration. Revisit the painting another time and review your impression of it:

▶ Has your opinion or feeling about it changed at all?
▶ On looking again at it, do you notice anything you didn't before?

As we find out more about something and learn about our response, the growing breadth of our knowledge often enables us to better understand what we see. With that knowledge and understanding, appreciation often develops whether or not we like the work any better. But in my experience, often the more I learn and become familiar with, say, music, the more I discover in it to like.

Knowledge and understanding may also let us recognize new facets or layers. For instance, a good book or fine wine may have many layers which we appreciate only as our proficiency in reading or tasting increases.

There's also an element of giving ourselves up to an experience. As I grew up, I found opera difficult and rather thought it was an over-stylized lot of warbling. But when I went to the opera for the first time I fortunately decided to lay my prejudice and preconceptions aside and let the whole new experience wash over me. It was *La traviata* and, like the character played by Julia Roberts in the film *Pretty Woman* years later, I found myself, just like her, overwhelmed with the joy of the beauty of the music and whole experience at the same time as being transfused with the sorrow of the story. Nowadays, if I want to fire up my creativity, I have only to listen to music I adore, including opera, and passion and inspiration flow.

> **Insight**
> The arts and other people's creativity generally are a great catalyst for our own individual creativity. It flows whenever we take a keen interest in something, learn more about it and appreciate the way we resonate with the ideas in it and the spirit and inspiration behind it.

How being imaginative and optimistic about your creativity really does light up your life

How can you dare to be creative? How can you dare not to be? It's such a big part of you that, if you repress it, you'll be repressing yourself. Recognize it, pay attention to it, love it and thereby encourage it to flow and it will be a fantastic part of you and your life. Your creativity is part of your truth and your being. It's also there to help you cope with life, and in any situation you can call on it by asking:

▶ How can I/we look at this situation in a different way?
▶ How can we address it in a *better* way?

- How can we encourage everyone involved to be equally positive, imaginative and constructive?
- How can we breathe liveliness and enthusiasm into the situation so that it's a feel-good experience for everyone?

Here are some possible answers:

- **Question and keep questioning.** Sometimes the old way is still the best way; sometimes we won't come up with good ideas. But if we're curious explorers with the optimism of pioneers, we'll seek out and see any opportunities, seize the ones we believe have legs and run with them.
- **Don't waste anything.** Everyone you meet will have their own characteristics, a particular way of talking, a certain light in their eye, their own set of beliefs and attitudes. Everything you see or otherwise sense from the earth below to the sky above is amazing; ask yourself how it came into being and if it has any relevance for you. Relish your thoughts: among the minutiae will be some interesting and original possibilities. Give them wings.
- **Look for the good to inspire you,** and, instead of letting the bad drag you down, think of it as part of life's rich compost that helps you grow your experience and develop.
- **Participate.** If you can't in actuality, you can in your mind. For instance, you may not have the chance to be a film producer or director, but you can read a novel or come up with your own story and imagine the film, set by set, character by character. Whom would you cast? How would you shoot it? What music would you have?

> Try this
> **Think of a word and use it for inspiration.** Don't fret that you may not come up with an interesting word; your mind will give you one that your imagination will be thrilled with. For instance, let's suppose the word 'camel' pops into your mind. You could write a short (or, if you wish, long) poem. Or imagine how you could get to know camels in some way – go on a walking holiday in Morocco, for instance, and visit the camel fair, or plan a trip to a wildlife park here in UK. Or you could draw or paint a camel. Don't fret that you haven't the skill – your creativity will provide.

This reminds me of a holiday in North Africa with an art school when we spent a day sketching at the camel fair. Everyone else was producing amazing drawings, but could I draw a camel? No! Eventually I was about to throw in the towel, convinced I simply didn't have the ability. 'I'll give it one more go,' I thought to myself. And as though independently of me, creativity flowed through my fingers, and through the charcoal and pastels they held, to produce one of the best drawings I've ever done. Yes, it was naive, but it was a camel through and through: I like to think the spirit of the beautiful, majestic animal connected with mine and inspired my creativity to flow. You, too, can practise, persist and let your creativity flow.

Listen for your soul's music

Remember to use free-flow writing or painting, meditation, conversation with others – all of these and any other muse you wish – to contemplate and help figure out who you are. Not what you own and not necessarily what you do, but the essence of *you* – made manifest now, at this moment, on this earth, in this place.

How astonishing is that? Your presence.

And, even more astonishing, realize that you have your own innate creativity which is a part of your being and, like your fingerprint, unique to you. Let it thrive. If you know there is something you long to do, choose one or some of these phrases below as your mantra:

- ▶ Begin it.
- ▶ Just do it.
- ▶ Be the captain of your ship; set the course, take the wheel and steer your life!
- ▶ Harness the energy you need.
- ▶ Be the self you know you are and long to be.
- ▶ Paint your life and step into the picture.
- ▶ Say 'Yes!'
- ▶ Do it now.
- ▶ Take a first step, however small.
- ▶ Make a footprint.
- ▶ Shine!

Reach out to others in your own creative way and touch them with your verve and happiness

Whenever you allow and encourage yourself to give your creativity full rein to work its magic in your life, you tap into a rich seam of happiness, inspiration and love. When you reach out to others and connect with them, they sense this flowing and, if they wish, they can tap into it. Inspiration is deliciously infectious and it feels good to know you can stimulate others to be creative.

It's lovely when they bring their inspiration and energy to us, too. One of my neighbours came bouncing in the other day and said to me and another friend: 'I've had an idea. Let's all come up with five ideas for something creative and new. Then we can choose one or some of them and do it together!' As in our own individual ways we all lead full lives, this particular time we didn't come up with a viable idea for us all to join forces, but we did give ourselves fresh ideas for new projects. And her enthusiastic free flow of energy that morning lifted us all, both in the moment and for some time afterwards. And actually, as I'm remembering all this now, I'm reminding myself to take another look at my list…

Let's all be a muse for others. It's a gift to them and ourselves.

And who knows? Your inspiration could be a catalyst that makes a truly wonderful difference to someone or even saves their life. Far-fetched? Two people have told me that a man named Paul Newell, the therapist who gave them both counselling, helped them not just out of their deep depression but to find a new, fulfilling and comfortable direction in life. His approach was innovative, holistic and, coupled with his natural charisma, life-changingly creative. In all walks of life, creativity can work its magic.

Let your creativity flow out to others. Don't worry that you'll deplete your reserves – they are self-replenishing, with a little bit of help from you and your friends!

Creativity can also beneficially influence your behaviour towards others and your relationships with them in other ways. At any time, and sometimes from moment to moment, your conduct can change what's going on in your life. Imagination is crucial to the extent to which you are able to empathize with others. So if, instead of being self-centred, you imagine how they are feeling, you will also find it much easier to feel for them and be both empathic and sympathetic.

So at any time, with your imagination and therefore empathy as your guiding star, you can beneficially influence the way life unfolds in and around you.

The same is true of a group and, if anything, the power is intensified when you tune into and work with other like-minded souls:

> 'Never doubt that a small group of thoughtful committed citizens can change the world – it's the only thing that ever has.'
> Margaret Meade

That is true and so inspiring, but I would add again that *one* person can change the world, too! We can *all* make a difference.

On the radio I heard Rye Barcott recall giving Tabitha Atieno Festo a £10 grant to sell vegetables. When he returned to Africa the following summer she had started a medical clinic which today treats over 40,000 people a year. With Salim Mohamed they founded Carolina for Kibera in Kenya and are committed to helping the poor find the solutions to the problems they face. In the dedication to his co-founders in his book *It Happened on the Way to War: A Marine's Path to Peace*, Rye Barcott writes: 'Talent is universal but opportunity is not.' But he has seen how people in desperate places can take charge of their lives and create breathtaking change.

Thought, hand in hand with imagination, can lead to empathy and give birth to constructive ideas and planning. You may be able to act helpfully in several ways, using your creativity to…

- ▶ imagine you are shining a bright light into the various facets and elements of a problem
- ▶ look for a key to unlock a stuck situation
- ▶ think how you can change the atmosphere by your behaviour – it could be something as simple as a warm smile and changing your body language from negative to positive
- ▶ reflect on where you are now and finding a different route forward
- ▶ use your sixth sense to see what's wrong
- ▶ ask for healing – even if you don't believe in the power of prayer, it can still be powerful!
- ▶ imagine you have an angel looking after you
- ▶ look for inspiration and see if you can inspire others
- ▶ think how you can move more gracefully and, if necessary, faster
- ▶ think what the loving thing to do is

- ▶ turn to others' wisdom
- ▶ think how you can express yourself more clearly.

It also feels great to talk about others' creativity and share the pleasure it gives us. A book club where all the members have their turn at choosing the next book, emailing or talking about film or television dramas we've enjoyed, talking about any of the arts – such things draw us together and uplift us in shared inspiration. Reading poems aloud, singing... any way we express our appreciation of creativity feels wonderful and stands to inspire our own.

And millions of people are embracing the Internet's social platform websites where anyone can have their say, expressing opinions and creativity and feeling the energy of humankind and how good it is to share, debate and tell who we are and how we're feeling.

Insight

Our creativity is there to uplift us and generally does make us feel good. But the happiest creative people of all are those who use their creativity for the good of others. It could be anything from making something that gives others pleasure in some way, to reaching out to help them through your understanding and empathy.

You are never helpless. You can always make a difference.

The joy of recognizing and standing up for your true creative self

The more you think of yourself as creative, the more easily you will allow creativity to manifest itself in your life. An integral part of this recognition, for most of us, is to speak up – if not necessarily to others, then to ourselves.

> 'Men do not long continue to think what they have forgotten how to say.' C. S. Lewis

Forget or ignore your creative energy, need and ability, and it will shrink back to lie dormant deep within you. Tell yourself and others that you aren't creative, and you risk squashing it even more. Either way you may actually become convinced that you aren't creative. But all the time your creativity will be calling out to you, longing for you to remember it and to welcome it into your life.

When you listen to that longing and recognize that you *are* creative, and tell yourself and anyone interested so, you'll be blown away by the sense of coming home to the real you. So it's vital to *say* – or express in some other telling way – that you are creative. Our creativity loves it when we recognize and appreciate it and by doing so we enable it to flourish – and we flourish, too.

As you'll have seen throughout this book, and as you hopefully will remember for all time, there are many ways to let it spark into life and flow. But it helps so much to first *acknowledge* your creativity. Then you can think: 'What do I need to do today to let it through and to express it?'

Speak of your creativity, show it and, above all, treasure it.

Never, ever deny it. It is one of your greatest blessings.

Let it out and let it flow!

The synchronicity of creativity

There is a synchronicity when we are creative. Mind dovetails with inspiration and, fired by energy (and often it doesn't take much), the molten gold of creative expression starts to flow.

You can help the whole process by encouraging it every step of the way. If ever you're devoid of inspiration, open this book at random to remind yourself that you are creative and follow one or two of the exercises and tips, or simply let your train of thought pick up on mine and inspire you to be creative in your own special way.

To feel the thrill of your creativity:

▶ Sense it now – perhaps like energy tingling gently across your shoulders.
▶ Does it suggest where it wants to go? Or do you have an idea already and want to lead it?
▶ Just as a painter chooses a colour, loads a brush with it and makes a first mark, so you can then make a first step in your creative process.
▶ One step and you're started.
▶ Another and another and momentum builds.

▶ Feel the flow of your creativity and enjoy it to the full.
▶ Remember – always – to give thanks.

And remember, too:

▶ It's up to you to pay attention and notice the feeling when creativity sparks and flows. It feels right – as though it's at home with you, at one with you and, at the same time, at one with the universe.
▶ It isn't about celebrity or financial success, or a matter of fashion and luck. Your creativity is a part of you; an alchemy of ability and energy that in so many ways sings *of* you – the real, wonderful, unique you.
▶ Life is all about stories. Each of us has our own life story that comprises any number of situations and relationships as the years pass. And each one of us is part of the story and the history of this extraordinary world.
▶ Creativity weaves through all these stories, giving shape, texture and colour to our lives. It takes in, for example, our personalities, relationships, parenthood, grandparenthood, our myriad abilities, work and leisure, our emotions and the way we cope.

Insight

Sometimes we're moved by real stories, sometimes by fictional ones, and when a story strikes a chord we have a powerful feeling of connecting with others, with our own and universal emotions and with the golden seam of creativity, the energy that runs through us and the world.

Your story is unfolding, day by day. Your creativity is a fundamental part of it and, recognized and appreciated, it will help uplift you and show you the way along your path. Creative ideas, solutions and inspirations may come to us at any time. Like a breath of fresh air, a flash of silver, a shooting star – suddenly it's there in your mind. And when creative energy flows, it lifts and carries you along and you feel: 'Yes – this is how it's meant to be and how I am meant to be.'

When we harmonize with our creativity it's a wonderful feeling.

You are already there, in tune. I wish you excitement, fulfilment, happiness and peace.

6 POINTS OF REFLECTION

1 When you've done something creative – even if it's a first step into it – feel how satisfying it is. Fulfilment is one of the great rewards of creativity and it's always there if we let it come through and don't suppress it.

2 Remember that being creative is very much a matter of habit. The more often you think or behave or paint or do anything creative, the easier it becomes and the more often you'll want to do it. Make being creative your way of life.

3 Take a vibrant interest in your creativity. Why not? It's a vital part of you and it feels wonderful.

4 Remember to cherish your imagination and your optimism – your appreciation will pay dividends in your creative flow.

5 Every day nurture your creativity in some way – and preferably in lots of ways! Some free-flow writing, meditation, brainstorming, making a collage – anything that appeals at that moment.

6 Share the magic of your creativity with others and take joy in theirs. Rejoice in your creativity and the way it flows and how good it feels. Love the way you harmonize and synchronize with it. When you do you are at one with the world.

Taking it further

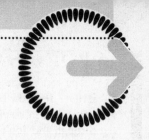

Books

These are books that have inspired me in the past, many of which I dip into again whenever I need inspiration or a feeling of solidarity with other creative people.

Julia Cameron, *The Artist's Way* (Pan).

Michele Cassou and Stewart Cubley, *Life, Paint and Passion* (Tarcher/Penguin).

Annie Dillard, *The Writing Life* (HarperPerennial).

Betty Edwards, *Drawing with the Right Side of the Brain* (HarperCollins).

Frederick Franck, *The Zen of Seeing* (Vintage).

Donald Friedman, *The Writer's Brush* (Mid-List Press).

Shakti Gawain, *Living in the Light* (New World Library).

Natalie Goldberg, *Living Colour* (Bantam).

Natalie Goldberg, *Wild Mind: Living the Writer's Life* (Rider).

David Hockney, *That's the Way I See It* (Thames and Hudson).

Ted Hughes, *Poetry in the Making* (Faber).

Stephen King, *On Writing: A Memoir of the Craft* (New English Library).

Gordon Lamont, *The Creative Path* (Azure).

Penny Stanway, *Free Your Inner Artist* (Stobart Davies).

Any books by Mihaly Csikszentmihalyi or C. S. Lewis

Websites

If you have any favourites that you rate highly and visit often as a source of inspiration and ideas, please let me know. Here are mine:

www.pennystanway.com   My sister's website – she is a wonderfully inspired artist and always so generously inspiring to other creative people.

www.jeanettewinterson.com   The website of author Jeanette Winterson is as inspiring and thought-provoking as her books.

www.michelecassou.com   Whenever I read one of Michele Cassou's books or visit her website it resonates with me joyously and inspires me to be creative.

www.marianne.com   In her books and website Marianne Williamson always makes me think: 'Yes – of course – we can make choices and we can all make a difference... me too!'

www.spiritofhorse.com   Kim McElroy writes and paints like a dream and her work is so uplifting.

www.shaktigawain.com   Shakti Gawain's books and now her website continue to be a huge inspiration to me many years ago as I follow my creative path.

Last but not least, I hope you enjoy visiting my website www.jennyhare.com. I hope my enthusiasm and inspiration shine through it. If you've any thoughts for the Art-Oasis section, please email them to me via the site.

Index

affirmation, *34–6*
anger, *63, 65, 112*
appreciation, *31–3, 56*
artistic ability, *3*
attitudes, *46–57, 161*
    curiosity, *52–4*
    developing a creative attitude,
      49–51
    and imagination, *120*
    original thinking, *46–8*

Ballesteros, Seve, *56*
Barcott, Ray, *170*
beauty, *157–8*
blocks to creativity, *71–3*
board games, *52*
books, *12, 82, 152*
boredom, *120–2*
the brain, *18, 104–16*
    and drawing, *104–7*
    and emotions, *111–14*
    focusing, *37–8*
    left brain function, *114, 115*
    right brain function, *6, 105–6,*
      107–9, 115
    and silence, *84*
brainstorming, *90–1*
breathing, *14, 54*
Broca, Pierre Paul, *106*

card games, *52*
challenges, *41–2*
children, *19, 118, 164*
confidence, *67*
the countryside, *27–8*
creativity statements, *4–5*
criticism, *65–6*
    others' negativity, *100–2*
    and self-esteem, *61–2*
    subjective, *42–4*
curiosity, *52–4, 145*

dancing, *81, 94*
day boards, *23, 83*
daydreaming, *2, 35*
depression, *65–7, 153*
discussion, *48*
drawing and the brain, *104–7*

education, *46–7, 69–70*
Edwards, Betty, *105*
Elgar, Edward, *85*
email correspondence, *48*
emotions
    and the brain, *111–14*
    and the creative process, *142*
    negative, *62–5*
    of other people, *153*
    positive, *67*
    and the senses, *156*
encouragement, *31–45*
    and appreciation, *31–3*
    focusing, *36–40*
    self-belief, *33–6, 39–40*
energy levels, *68*
enjoyment, *56–7, 133–4, 138–42*
envy, letting go of, *73*
equipment, *80*
everyday activities, *7, 12–13, 17,*
    18–20, 158–9
exercise, *24, 68, 81, 84*
    with others, *93–4*
experience and practice, *9–10*

fear, *63*
films, *82, 82–3, 97*
finances, *41, 70–1*
flow of creativity, *127–8, 133, 138,*
    151–2
    free-flowing writing, *20–3, 39,*
      162, 168
    and the senses, *156*
focusing, *36–8, 91*

food, *68, 69*
free-flowing writing, *20–3, 39, 162, 168*
friendships, *19*
fulfilment of living creatively, *161–2*

games, *52, 93–4*
gathering information, *3*
Geldof, Bob, *67*
geniuses, *5*
guilt, *63–4*
gurus, *11–12, 25–6*

habit and creativity, *12, 162–3*
Hancock, Tony, *97*
healing power of being creative, *143–4*
health, *68–71*
hidden creativity, *13*
hobbies, *19*
homes and domestic creativity, *19, 147–8*
hope, *67*

ideas, *3*
imagination, *1–2, 117–20, 166–8*
    and others' creativity, *170–1*
imaging, *98–9*
individual creativity, *2, 96–100*
individual slants, *3*
information
    gathering and sorting, *3*
ingenuity, *2*
insight, *3*
inspiration, *3, 7, 67, 129–30*
    and other people, *152–4*
    and words, *167–8*
    see also muses
inspirational outings, *80–1*
intuition, *7–9, 162–3*
invention, *2–3*

jealousy, letting go of, *73*
journal keeping, *20*

Kant, Immanuel, *61*

laughter, *25, 95–6, 164*
learning, *9, 69–70*
    ongoing, *164–6*
leisure activities, *19, 149–52*
letting in the light of creativity, *16–18*
Lewis, C. S., *12, 82, 171*
lifestyle, *147–60*
listening
    creatively, *26–7, 155–5*
    to other people, *88–90*
logic and creativity, *6*
looking, *27–8, 156*
love, *56, 112, 134, 148, 154, 162*

McCall, Kenneth, *148–9*
Meade, Margaret, *170*
meditation, *7–8, 39, 85, 123–6, 129*
    and the brain, *107–8*
meeting people *see* personal contacts
mental health, *68*
mentors, *11, 41*
mindful living, *13–14, 162*
money, *41, 70–1*
muses, *6, 7, 23, 75–85*
    creative media, *82–3*
    inspirational outings, *80–1*
    personal contacts, *85–6, 169–71*
    pets, *86*
    place, *77–80*
    silence and solitude, *84–5*
    time, *75–7*
music, *7, 26, 94–5*

negativity
    negative emotions, *62–5*
    other people's, *100–1*
notebooks, *23–4, 83*

oases of creativity, *154–5*
optimism, *67, 166–8*
original thinking, *2, 46–8*
outings, inspirational, *80–1*

painting, *8, 31–2, 42, 104*
    and negative emotions, *62–3*
    'splodging', *150–1*
paintings, *43, 82–3*
parenting, *41*
partnerships, creative, *91–3*
passion, *51*
personal contacts, *81, 85–6, 88–103*
    and creative inspiration, *152–4*
    creative partnerships, *91–3*
    exercise, sports and games,
      93–4
    and laughter, *95–6*
    listening and talking to people,
      88–90
    music and dancing, *94–5*
    other people's negativity, *100–2*
    reaching out to others, *169–71*
    team work, *90–1*
pets, *19, 24, 86*
Picasso, Pablo, *85*
places, *77–80, 154–6*
planning projects, *3*
play, *24–5, 51–2*
positive emotions, *67*
positive thinking, *60*
practice and experience, *9–10*
problem-solving, *17–18*
process of creativity, *132–45*
    engaging in the process, *135–6*
    enjoyment of the, *138–42*
    healing power of being creative,
      143–4
    starting the process, *136–8*
projects, planning, *3*

questioning, *167*

The Rebel, *97*
relationships, *8–9, 85–6*
    creative partnerships, *91–3*
relaxation, *54–5, 84, 85*
resentment, *64*
rewards, *12*

scents, *28–9, 155*
scrapbooks, *23–4, 83*
seeing, *27–8, 156*
self-belief, *33–6, 39–40, 98*
self-doubt, *19–20*
self-esteem, *59–62, 135*
    and lifestyle, *147–8*
the senses, *6–7, 26–9*
    using to enhance creativity,
      155–6
sensual ability, *3*
seven principles of creativity,
    38–9
sexual attraction and desire, *156*
sexuality, *112*
silence, *84–5*
singing, *81*
sketch pads, *23–4*
smell, *28–9, 155*
solitude, *84–5*
sorting information, *3*
sources of creativity, *5–10*
space, lack of, *40*
Sperry, Roger, *106*
spirituality, *10, 126–8*
sports, *93–4*
Stanway, Penny, *33*
subjective criticism, *42–4*
synchronicity of creativity, *172–3*

talent, *13*
taste, *29, 155*
teachers, *11–12, 25–6*
team work, *90–1*
technical skills, *69–70*
'thinking out of the box', *3*
time
    giving yourself time to think,
      48
    lack of, *40–1*
    muse, *75–7*
    personal time and the
      imagination, *119–20*
Tolkien, J. R. R., *12*

touch, *29*, *156*
training and learning, *9*
travel, *85*
troubleshooting, *17–18*

uniqueness, *157–8*

Van Gogh, Vincent, *43–4*

visualization, *34–7*, *108*, *125–6*

water, *28*
'what's right' mindset, *55–6*
willingness, *56*
workplace creativity, *19*, *90–1*
writing
    free-flowing, *20–3*, *39*, *162*, *168*